boundless Love

Devotions to Celebrate
God's Love for You

WOMEN OF FAITH™

PATSY CLAIRMONT   BARBARA JOHNSON
MARILYN MEBERG   LUCI SWINDOLL
SHEILA WALSH   THELMA WELLS

boundless *Love*

Devotions to Celebrate
God's Love for You

TRACI MULLINS, GENERAL EDITOR

ZONDERVAN™

GRAND RAPIDS, MICHIGAN 49530 USA

ZONDERVAN™

Boundless Love
Copyright © 2001 by Women of Faith, Inc.

Requests for information should be addressed to:

Zondervan, *Grand Rapids, Michigan 49530*

ISBN 0-310-25981-9

This is a custom edition for Man in the Mirror.

Published in association with the literary agency of Alive Communications, Inc., 7680 Goddard Street, Suite 200, Colorado Springs, CO 80920.

"Oh the Passion" by Gary Sadler and David Boroni © 2000 Integrity's Hosanna! Music/ASCAP & Integrity's Praise! Music/BMI. All rights reserved. International copyright secured. Used by permission.

All Scripture quotations, unless otherwise indicated, are taken from the *Holy Bible: New International Version*®. NIV®. Copyright © 1973, 1978, 1984 by International Bible Society. Used by permission of Zondervan. All rights reserved.

Other Scripture quotations are from *New American Standard Bible* (NASB), © 1960, 1977 by the Lockman Foundation; *The Message* (MSG), © 1993, 1994, 1995 by Eugene H. Peterson; *The Living Bible* (TLB), © 1971 by Tyndale House Publishers; The New Living Translation (NLT), © 1996 By Tyndale Charitable Trust; and the *King James Version* (KJV).

Interior design by Nancy Wilson

Printed in the United States of America

04 05 06 07 08 09 10 / ❖ OPM / 10 9 8 7 6 5 4 3 2 1

Contents

~ Lavish Love ~

~ Outlandish Love ~

~ Intentional Love ~

Introduction:
Evidence to the Contrary

~ Marilyn Meberg

Southern writer Flannery O'Connor once said she thinks the South is more Christ-haunted than Christ-centered. She implies that the Southern belief system may spring from a type of fearful superstition rather than a solid faith. Since the word *superstition* is defined as "a belief held in spite of evidence to the contrary," I wonder if many of us, no matter what our geographic origins, may not fall into the category of being Christ-haunted more frequently than we're Christ-centered.

Quite frankly, as I wrote that last sentence I found myself slightly offended. *For heaven's sake . . . of course I'm not merely Christ-haunted. I have a solid, Christ-centered core!* But here's the thought that gives me pause: I do indeed have a Christ-centered core, simply because the Spirit of God lives within me. But occasionally, unconsciously, I can attach a type of superstitious thinking to my faith.

For example, maybe the reason I got an unexpected check for $100 is that I've been reading my Bible more. Or, maybe the reason my health problems persist is that I'm not tithing enough. Possibly the reason the windows in my new condo leak when it rains is that I didn't pray enough for guidance before I bought it.

These are not faith-based thoughts; they are superstitious thoughts. They are on the same level of thinking as, *If I do not walk under that ladder I'll meet a gorgeous man who finds me irresistible. Of course, if I do walk under that ladder . . . well, prepare to meet Phantom of the Opera.*

Superstitious thinking leads me to believe that if I increase my prayer time, Bible study, tithing, and "good works" across the board,

I will win more of God's favor, and as a result, my circumstances will get better. On the other hand, when things go badly (poor health, no unexpected checks, leaky windows, and the Phantom takes up residence in my attic), there must be something I'm doing wrong. Then I may cast about, searching for the formula that "works," because what I'm currently doing is not working according to my preconceived ideas of what is "good." When I think like this, I may be reducing God to a good-luck charm, which I think I can rub like a rabbit's foot when I need him.

When we find ourselves falling into a formula-seeking kind of living, then we, as the definition for *superstition* states, are holding onto "a belief in spite of evidence to the contrary." So what's the evidence to the contrary? The evidence is simply and profoundly: God loves you; God loves me.

The evidence of God's love was exhibited to us in the flesh when Jesus walked this earth to make his Father known and to die for the sins of humankind. The fact of his boundless, fearless, stubborn, lavish, outlandish, intentional love is not based upon whether we read our Bibles, tithe "enough," buy a condo with bad windows, or walk under ladders. His very nature is love, and we are the objects of that love. Believing *that* evidence provides the "formula" for living our lives with joy and purpose.

The six of us have written on the colossal subject of God's love with tremendous joy and deep humility. As you read the personal perspective and experience of each of us on this stunning dimension of God, our prayer, like the apostle Paul's before us, is that "with both feet planted firmly on love, you'll be able to take in with all Christians the extravagant dimensions of Christ's love. Reach out and experience the breadth! Test its length! Plumb the depths! Rise to the heights! Live full lives, full in the fullness of God" (Ephesians 3:17–18 MSG).

Boundless
Love

Dearest Reader,

"Come on, Marilyn — get your face under water. You can't miss this!" My husband Ken's goggled face popped up out of the Caribbean waters of Cozumel, Mexico, as he shouted with glee.

I had reluctantly agreed to go snorkeling, but I'd hoped that somehow I could snorkel without getting too wet and certainly without total submersion into waters I did not trust. I had thus far proven to be a less-than-fun snorkel date, but determined to join Ken in something that was giving him such pleasure, I forced myself to get my face under water.

I was stunned! There were at least a bizillion (conservative estimate) brilliantly colored fish zipping enthusiastically in all directions. It was as if I had been dropped into an enormous aquarium with no sides and no bottom. Ken and I were soon popping to the surface shouting our enthusiasm to each other before diving back into the kaleidoscopically beautiful underwater world I might have missed because I didn't want to get my face wet.

As you begin reading about God's boundless love, you may be stunned as you realize that his love has no sides and no bottom. It just goes on forever! Let me encourage you to go ahead and get your face all the way under the water. Patsy, Barbara, Luci, Thelma, Sheila, and I will be swimming along right beside you. Let's immerse ourselves in the vastness of God's "You don't want to miss this" love!

Love,

Marilyn

Imagine That!

~ Patsy Clairmont

Two days ago I was sitting in a hospital lounge waiting for our first grandchild to be born. No, let me restate that. I was *not* sitting; I was pacing. Back and forth, back and forth, attentively listening for a tiny cry or footsteps of someone, anyone, bearing good news. I was both excited and exhausted as the hours ticked by . . . five hours, seven hours, nine hours, and then finally, Justin Robert Clairmont was born! He was seven pounds, thirteen ounces, and twenty-two inches long with red hair. Yes-s-s!

After word arrived that all was well, we four grandparents waited with bated breath for our first glimpse of this child who would forever hold our hearts in his hands. That's when I saw a picture that I'll always think of as expressing God's boundless love. The surgery doors swung open (our daughter-in-law had an emergency cesarean), and I saw Jason, my youngest son, walking toward me carrying his firstborn son. My baby was carrying his baby. Wow!

If ever we doubt God's love, we need only observe a baby we deeply care for and then take the feelings of love that bubble up in our hearts and multiply them by infinity. Then we'll have a sense—just a sense, mind you—of God's boundless love.

I find that imagining the vastness of God's love is as close as I can come to measuring it. Perhaps that's why, when the Lord designed us, he included our capacity for imagination. He knew we wouldn't "get it" if we had to weigh his love next to our own puny experiences and abilities to love. He knew we would need to think beyond ourselves and so—*voila!*—imagination.

Some of my favorite "imagining" verses are found in Job 38 in which the Lord expands Job's mind with thoughts beyond himself. God quizzes Job as to his whereabouts when God created the universe in order to help Job understand the Lord's majestic spaciousness.

"Where were you when I laid the foundation of the earth?"
—Job 38:4 NASB

This absolute statement of proclamation could read, "I laid the foundation of the world before you were a sparkle in your momma's eye!"

Can you visualize laying the earth's foundation? Les and I just purchased a home that is being built, but by the time we made the decision to buy, the foundation already had been poured and the walls were up. Even though I can picture the big excavation trucks digging out the hole, the cement truck pouring the footings and foundation, and the bricklayers building the walls for our home, I can't conceive of how one would go about laying the world's foundation. You would need a cement mixer the size of the Western Hemisphere!

"Where were you [Job] . . . when the morning stars sang together, and all the sons of God shouted for joy?"
—Job 38:4, 7 NASB

Can you conceive of the morning stars singing? I love all kinds of music: Celine Dion, Michael Bolton, Andrea Bocelli, Mandy Patinkin, The Martins . . . Music moves me. I mean, have you heard Mandy Patinkin sing "Over the Rainbow"? Exquisite. I cry almost every time I hear it. Or have you heard Celine Dion and Luciano Pavarotti sing "I Hate You Then I Love You"? Oh, mama mia! And yet I'm certain that, if we teamed up all these gifted singers for one grand performance, they would not, could not, hold a candle to the concert of the morning stars. Of course, I, like Job, wasn't there for the performance, so I'm left imagining.

"Have you [Job] ever in your life commanded the morning, and caused the dawn to know its place?"
—Job 38:12 NASB

I commanded my children when they were young (now they command me), and according to Les, I've commanded him a time or two, but I confess I wouldn't begin to know how to give instruction to the morning or the dawn. At times I've wanted to call off a day, but alas, I didn't have that kind of celestial clout.

Our magnificent God, however, knows the beginning, the end, and beyond. He calls the stars by name, and he has planned and recorded each and every day—including the day my first grandson was born. Imagine that!

Now that, folks, is boundless—boundless love.

"This is love: not that we loved God, but that he loved us and sent his Son as an atoning sacrifice for our sins" (1 John 4:10). Imagine that!

Hosanna the Donkey

~ Sheila Walsh

Miss Dawn is my hero. Twice a week she takes care of a roaming pack of three-year-olds at Christ Presbyterian Academy's Toddler Time. She is smiling when we arrive at 9:10 A.M., and then, as if to serve as visual proof of the existence of God, she is still smiling at 2:15 P.M. when the day ends. Our son, Christian, loves her. When he prays for her at night he goes all mushy. What a gift from God when your child's first teacher is such a sweetheart.

Each time Christian gets out of school I check his lunch box to see if he has eaten any of his lunch. Usually he just rearranges it. Then I read his "What kind of day I had today" sheet. It's almost always the same:

> Christian had a good day today. He participated in everything and was very communicative [just like his dad]. He didn't eat much and didn't take his nap, but he lay quietly like a good boy, occasionally whispering to his rabbit, Whitey.

My desk is covered with things Christian has made at school. A manger made out of graham crackers. A tulip made from his handprint cut out of pink paper and folded in like petals. A jewelry box in the shape of a cross which he presented to me with the matter-of-fact statement, "Jesus died for your sins and this is for your rings." So I knew that during Easter week Miss Dawn was sharing more than just the Easter Bunny with her pint-size boys and girls.

My son, being a typical male, does not always give me all the information I'd like at the end of each school day. Still, I try.

"How was school today?"

"Fine."

"What did you learn?"

"Nothing."

"Did you sing?"

"No."

"Did you play outside?"

"No."

"So you just sat around for five hours and did nothing?"

". . . Did you say something, Mommy?"

I've learned that the best way to get Christian to "spill his stuff" is to go bike riding together. So every evening he and I mount up and head for the hills, and you wouldn't believe what I learn as we kick up dust together.

The evening before Good Friday we were pushing our bikes back into the garage when he said, "You know, Mom, today when I was Jesus riding into Jerusalem on a donkey, Tristan and Zachary waved branches to say hello. It was cool."

"You were Jesus?" I asked, wondering at Miss Dawn's discernment as she cast the roles.

"Sure! Hey, you want me to do it for Daddy and Papa?" he asked, full of joy at the thought of an encore performance.

We went inside and announced that the show was about to begin. That's not unusual in our household. We have frequent performances. Sometimes they're from *Mary Poppins* or *The Wizard of Oz*. This, however, was our first biblical epic. Christian and I hid behind the door leading into the kitchen where Barry and William, Christian's grandpa, waited in eager (?) expectation.

"Okay," Christian said. "I'll be Jesus and you be Hosanna."

"What do you mean?" I asked. "Who's Hosanna?"

"Well, the donkey, of course!" he said, looking at me as if I had temporarily backslidden.

"Why do you think the donkey's name is Hosanna?"

"Mommy, think about it. I'm Jesus, right?"

"Right."

"Well, as I'm coming in they all shout, 'Hosanna!' That's not me. That has to be you."

I tried to explain that "Hosanna!" is a cry of praise and adoration, that it was directed toward Jesus. He listened intently and then announced, "Okay, Hosanna. We're on."

As we reenacted that joyful scene in the Gospels, I thought about how dreadful it is that so many of those who exuberantly cried, "Hosanna to the One who comes in the name of the Lord!" also cried out, "Crucify him!" just a few days later. And I wonder if we as human beings have changed much in the two thousand years since those fickle cries sent Jesus to the cross. If you are like me, you often feel like two people. Some days we live in such a way that our actions cry out praise to God. But on other days it's as if we crucify Christ all over again.

The most wonderful thing about the love of God expressed in Christ is that none of this is a surprise to him. God entrusted his Son to a harsh, cruel world knowing that it would first embrace him and then spit on him and kill him. And yet he did it anyway—because his love has no limits. God's love cannot be quenched by the ever-turning tides of human emotion and devotion.

If I could say only one thing through my part of this book, it would be simple and to the point: God knows all about you. He knows your good days and your bad days. He knows the noble thoughts and the shameful thoughts. He sees your devotion and your indifference. And he loves you—totally, completely, passionately, boundlessly. Forever.

> Oh the Passion, Oh the wonder,
> Of the fiery love of Christ.
> King of Glory on the altar. Perfect lamb of sacrifice.
> Who are we that he would love us? Who but he
>   would give his life?
> Oh the Passion, Oh the wonder,
> Of the fiery love of Christ.

Oh the wisdom, Oh the wonder,
Of the power of the cross.
Love so rare no words could tell it. Life himself has
   died for us.
Who are we that he would save us? Crucified to
   give us life?
Oh the wisdom, Oh the wonder,
Of the power of the cross.

—*Sheila Walsh*

You are loved! You are loved
passionately and unconditionally
by the God who gave his only
Son so you could rest secure
in his eternal embrace.

The Boy Next Door

~ Marilyn Meberg

She had *what?*"

"Ruptured silicone implants."

"What did she do?"

"Had 'em taken out."

"So other than her being flat-chested, what's the problem?"

"A bunch of physical symptoms. At first a doctor summed it up by telling her she had an immune disorder but didn't know its cause."

"What does that have to do with silicone implants?"

"She later learned that apparently silicone is toxic."

"I read that it isn't."

"She read the same thing."

"So what's the deal with her?"

"She's getting better; the improvements are slow, but they're happening."

That mini-dialogue about me has occurred to varying degrees between various people who have known something was "off" with me, but didn't know what. For a while I didn't know what either. One sure way to put someone into a coma is to launch into a detailed health report, so I'll spare you that. I do, however, want to discuss my personal experience because almost everything I write in this book springs from what God is teaching me in it. But before we get too spiritual, I'll pull aside the privacy curtain and tell you how all this came about in the first place.

Twenty-eight years ago my neighbor, Mary, dashed across the street to tell me she was getting a fantastic deal on silicone implants from the plastic surgeon for whom she worked.

"But," I said, "isn't his specialty noses? He fixes noses, not bosoms."

"I guess he wanted to branch out or something. Anyway, he took the training, he's certified, board approved, and I'm losing my boy-next-door look in the morning!"

Having sported the boy-next-door look myself as long as I could remember, I was envious.

"So how come you're getting a deal, Mary. What does that mean?"

"Well, my doctor needs the experience, so I get the surgery at his cost. He told me he would offer the same deal to a few of my friends if they were interested."

That evening I brought up the subject to Ken, who was mildly horrified by the "I'll give you a deal while I learn the procedure" mentality. I pointed out to Ken that there was some similarity in the shapes of noses and bosoms and maybe it wasn't really such a stretch to move from the nose to the . . . Ken was not convinced.

Because I couldn't rid myself of the appeal of sporting feminine curves instead of boyish lines, Ken did some investigating about Mary's doctor and learned he had impeccable credentials, as well as an excellent reputation with other doctors. With Ken's reluctant approval I had the breast surgery done by the nose man.

The results were exceedingly gratifying. Even Ken became an enthusiast. (I must admit, however, that the flaring little nostrils at the base of each breast were a bit distracting.) The reality is, I had no problems with them at all. In contrast, a friend of mine paid a breast augmentation specialist four times what I did and had to have the surgery redone twice. The first time, one breast pointed slightly north and the other south. The second time, they both pointed a little south. I told her she should have hired a nose man.

Seven months ago, I yielded to the persistent nagging of my OB-GYN and got a mammogram. (I had not had one in twenty years . . . I was afraid that Gestapo technique might cause my noses to run.) With ill-disguised horror, the doctor showed me on a sonogram that both implants were ruptured and that my chest cavity was full of free-floating silicone. She told me to "run, not walk" to a surgeon for removal of the mess.

Assuming that my task was merely to get the operation and return to boyishness, I was stunned to learn that my entire body was splattered with stray silicone—the greatest concentration being in the lymph nodes under both arms. While there are many women with silicone implants who have no symptoms of toxicity, my recovery from all that floating poison, in spite of the removal of the implants, has proven to be slow and, at times, debilitating.

My intent in writing this is not to become a poster child for silicone survivors. Silicone, whether it is indeed toxic or not, is a subject of medical controversy and increasingly serious inquiry as well as research. My intent is to provide background for some of the other things I've written in this book and, more important, to underscore the reality of God's boundless love in the midst of our messes in life.

It would make perfect sense to me if God's response to my current needs was expressed with statements like: "Well, Marilyn, after all, you brought this whole health crisis on yourself. You're simply experiencing the consequences of your own vanity, your poor decisions nearly thirty years ago. Here you are struggling with challenges that have their origin in your worldly, self-absorbed preoccupation with something as superficial as not wanting to look like the boy next door. Tsk, tsk, tsk."

Those messages, which I give myself, have never once been echoed by God. In stark contrast I consistently receive the encouragement and solace of his nonjudgmental love and support:

> I cried out, "I'm slipping!" and your unfailing love, O LORD, supported me.   —*Psalm 94:18* NLT

Nothing I have done as a faltering human being merits what I receive daily from him. He even says:

> The steps of the godly are directed by the LORD.
> He delights in every detail of their lives.

Though they stumble, they will not fall,
for the LORD holds them by the hand.

—*Psalm 37:23* NLT

What is so astounding to me is that God does not say, "As long as you don't stumble, Marilyn, I'll hang around and be supportive." Rather, he says he *delights* in every detail of my life—not because the details are always delightful but because he is my hand-holding God who walks with me through the events of my life no matter how foolish or misguided my steps may be. In fact, he uses those very experiences to deepen and strengthen my relationship with him. Scripture reminds me of why he cares so deeply about what is going on in my world.

The LORD still waits for you to come to him so he can show you his love and compassion. For the LORD is a faithful God. Blessed are those who wait for him to help them.

—*Isaiah 30:18* NLT

How blessed each of us is to have such a compassionate, faithful God! When we feel like we've made a mess of things (even if it's only by mistake), we can be sure that our ever-waiting Lord will not only remove the mess, but show us the fullness of his boundless love as we wait for rescue.

As for me, I thank God that many of my troublesome symptoms are beginning to lessen; my stamina and overall health are returning. No matter what the future holds, no matter what shape my body parts are in, I know God's love for me will never waver.

Flat or "busty" —
you are loved!

One Great Fellowship

~ Luci Swindoll

A Belgian poet once said that if the world is spherical, it is made that way so love and friendship and peace can go round it. I like that thought. And I've traveled enough to know there's truth to it. When we give love, it comes back to us; when we're friendly, others are friendly too; and when peace abounds, it reproduces itself. These are generalities, I know, but more often than not this has been my experience. What goes around comes around.

In February of last year a group of us from Women of Faith had the opportunity to go to West Africa. For six days, the president of Women of Faith, Mary Graham, its CEO, Stephen Arterburn, Thelma, her daughter Vikki, and I journeyed to Ghana with members of World Vision. World Vision is a relief organization that seeks to address the root causes of poverty, pooling money from sponsors to provide life-changing benefits—like safe water, agricultural assistance, medical care, educational assistance, spiritual support, whatever is necessary to help families become self-reliant. Women of Faith is one of several organizations that encourage people to give money in support of this cause. We were in Ghana to attend the inauguration of the Family Support Project, which, instead of supporting individual children as they've traditionally done, supports whole families. We were going to meet "our" families, who live in remote villages. This was a very interesting and wonderful opportunity to take love, friendship, and peace to the other side of the globe, and to receive the same from the people who live there.

One morning as we were meeting for breakfast, Vikki Wells gave a short devotional from Acts 4:32: "All the believers were one in heart and mind. No one claimed that any of his possessions was his own, but they shared everything they had."

Everybody standing in that circle, she said, was just the same in Christ. There were no differences or barriers. There were no degrees of separation because of race, color, status, background, possessions. *I love that*. We were indeed one great fellowship. Fellowship is a beautiful word. Who doesn't want to experience mutual sharing with those of like mind and heart?

Then Vikki concluded her thoughts with the first verse from an old hymn. We all sang it in our own languages.

> In Christ there is no east or west,
> In him no south or north;
> But one great fellowship of love
> Throughout the whole wide earth.

I remember thinking at that moment, *I'm over here on the other side of the globe, yet I feel so at home. At peace. Why do I feel this way? What is it?* It didn't take long to realize that "it" was spiritual companionship and shared passion for the same Savior. Although each of us was vastly different from the other on the outside, we were the same on the inside. There is no east nor west, no south nor north in Christ. He is the same gravitational point that draws all persons to himself. I celebrated that truth the entire time I was in Ghana. The differences between us simply didn't matter.

An interesting aside: while I was in Africa sharing Christ with the nationals there, my brothers were on two other continents doing the same—Orville in South America and Chuck in Asia. Three siblings who live in North America were taking love, peace, and friendship to opposite sides of the globe at the same time. I was thrilled when I realized that, because our mother taught us as children Jesus' words in Matthew 28:19–20: "Therefore go and make disciples of all nations, baptizing them in the name of the Father and of the Son and of the Holy Spirit, and teaching them to obey everything I have commanded you. And surely I am with you always, to the very end of the age." Here we were, decades later, living out our mother's greatest wish for us in Christ. *Mama, can you see me?* And Christ was with each of us even though we were miles apart.

The sweetest part of the relationship we have with the Almighty is telling others about what we've learned and that they, too, can enjoy oneness with God. They can know his love by becoming intimately acquainted with his Son, Jesus. Witnessing is not some hocus-pocus thing. It's simply showing up in life every day, expressing what God has done for us, how he's met us along the way, and how he can do the same for the person with whom we're sharing. Mother Teresa said, "Wherever God has put you, that is your vocation. It is not what we do but how much love we put into it." And, I figure, she should know.

I realize it's not possible for everybody to travel to a foreign country to share the gospel. That's not the point of Jesus' "great commission." The point is to simply *go*. Anywhere. To talk to anybody about the friendship God offers through the redemptive work of his Son on the cross. We don't need money or a passport, a vaccination or a plane ticket to fulfill the commission Jesus gave us. We don't have to speak another language to make the good news of Jesus Christ clear to someone who has never heard. What we need is a heart of love, which causes us to reach out in the first place.

It's not just that Belgian poet who encourages us to share friendship, love, and peace, but we have been summoned by the Savior himself to do it. We are commanded to introduce people to him, train them in the way they should live under his love and protection, instruct them in his teachings. And when we do this, he has promised us his constant presence. What could be more loving and fulfilling than such a powerful assignment and such a personal promise?

I don't have any way of knowing where you are as you're reading this, but wherever it is in the whole wide earth, please know you are loved by the God of the universe. He offers you friendship and peace. He wants to share with you everything he has! His fellowship reaches next door, down the street, through the city, over the plains, across the ocean, and around the world.

Look at a world map and remind yourself that Christ died for every person in every country. Including you. Including me. That was the greatest act of love — ever.

"They Call Me the Wanderer"

~ Sheila Walsh

I lost Lily again last night. It's the fourth time in a month. She hides in the linen closet or in the attic or under Christian's bed. The truth is, our cat, Lily, is a wanderer at heart.

I first saw her when she was in a little cage at the Nashville Humane Society. It was a weekend when Barry, William, and Christian were in Charleston, South Carolina, and I had stayed home to write. Barry and I have a kind of agreement that I won't visit the Humane Society by myself, but I don't find that agreement particularly binding. I try to avoid Harding Road, home of all waifs and strays, but when I'm by myself, it's hard.

That particular day I thought, *I'll just stop in and pet a few kitties and leave a donation for food and shelter.* Once I was there, however, something kicked in. I looked at all the cats in their cages looking so trapped and eager to be free. I scratched ears and sang little cat songs. Some stuck friendly paws through bars or purred like freshly tuned engines.

The only cat whose face I couldn't see was Lily's. She was sitting in her cage curled up in a basket, back to the world. I could tell that she was a beautiful cat. She was gold and white and had black markings on her long hair. I asked the attendant if I could take her out of her cage and hold her. I was told that I could at my own risk. I had no idea if she would bite me or throw up a hair ball on my new sweater. Instead she tucked her head under my arm and went to sleep.

Of course I took her home. I had two days to teach her the house rules before the boys returned. It was a piece of cake. She is the best cat in the world. She is more like a dog. She follows me everywhere I go. Barry was mad for a day, William was ecstatic, and Christian ran around the house crying out, "I have a sister! I have a sister!"

Lily's only little eccentricity is that she tends to wander. Most of the time I find her in one of her familiar hiding spots, but not last night. Everyone else was in bed. I was working late. So at about 2:00 A.M. I went to say good night to her before I turned in. No Lily. I looked everywhere. I checked all her usual camp-outs and came up empty.

After about an hour I knew she was not in the house. I got a flashlight and headed out into the backyard in my pajamas. Our house backs onto a golf course so there's a lot of ground to cover. I kept calling her name. "Lily! Lily! Where are you, you little monkey?" I knew I had to find her before morning. My neighbors have a gigantic Doberman pinscher, and Lily would be no more than a midmorning snack to Lular.

After thirty minutes of calling her name, I heard a faint meow. I kept calling her and walking toward the sound until I found her, hiding behind a bush. I picked her up and carried her home. She almost rubbed a hole in my leg she was so grateful to be safe, to be inside, to be back on familiar ground.

I thought about that as I lay in bed having fed her a celebratory can of tuna fish. I thought, *God is like that.* We all have wandering hearts. We all hide in closets or under beds and occasionally get outside a safe place . . . and time after time, God comes looking for us. There is nowhere that you can hide that the boundless love of God can't find you. No matter what kind of mess you get into, he'll be there.

Lily's paws were muddy and my pajamas were covered in dirt. How much more does God allow himself to be covered in our mud, our sin, our messes? But you'll never hear a word of complaint. Just a "Welcome home, you little monkey!"

Perhaps you feel as if you have gone too far. Let me assure you, you cannot go too far from God. Remember the words of that wonderful hymn written by a father who had lost everything he loved, apart from God: "Oh love that will not let me go." Not "could not let me go" but "will not let me go."

So when you hear that quiet call in your spirit in the darkest night of your life when you are lost beyond belief, just let out a little meow . . . and God will find you and carry you home and wash you off and feed you. He will always celebrate your return.

Even when we cross every boundary, God's boundless love finds us. We are never lost to God.

And Edith with Them

~ Barbara Johnson

D o you ever feel like you miss the point when it comes to God's love? The greatest love story ever told, the Bible, tells us repeatedly that his gracious love is a free gift from a devoted Father to a beloved child, an endless supply of everything we need to be secure and happy. And yet ... we miss the point. Like Jesus' devoted friend Martha, who found it so difficult simply to *accept* and *enjoy* his free and boundless love, we often scurry around in our endless activities *for* God and miss his ever-present love *for* us.

Not so with Edith. She got it, right from God's heart to hers.

Edith was a little girl who was an orphan on the streets of London after World War II. She would often sneak into the backs of public buildings to get warm, and one Sunday evening she slipped into the back of a church and listened to the sermon. How excited she was at what she heard!

As the congregation was filing out, shaking hands with the minister, the little girl rushed up to him and said, "Oh sir, sir, I'm so excited! I didn't know my name was in the Bible!"

The minister wracked his brain to recall mentioning a female's name in the text of his sermon, but he came up blank. Not wanting to hurt the little girl's feelings, he asked, "Well, honey, what *is* your name?"

"My name is Edith."

He was really confused now, and he *really* didn't want to hurt her feelings, but he had to admit that the name "Edith" does not occur in Scripture.

"But it does!" Edith said. "I heard you say it clearly tonight: 'Jesus receiveth sinners and Edith with them.'"

The minister chuckled as he reached out to stroke Edith's cheek. He had been preaching on Luke 15:2, where the Pharisees and religious teachers were complaining about how Jesus, the self-proclaimed holy man, spent time with sinners and "eateth" with them. (God forbid!) Little Edith may have misunderstood the word, but she certainly got the point! She heard the truth for her, for you, for me: the boundless love of God reaches out toward each and every one of us.

Jesus responded to the self-righteous Law-keepers with this parable:

> "Suppose one of you has a hundred sheep and loses one of them. Does he not leave the ninety-nine in the open country and go after the lost sheep until he finds it? And when he finds it, he joyfully puts it on his shoulders and goes home. Then he calls his friends and neighbors together and says, 'Rejoice with me; I have found my lost sheep.' I tell you that in the same way there will be more rejoicing in heaven over one sinner who repents than over ninety-nine righteous persons who do not need to repent."
> —*Luke 15:4–7*

He also proclaimed, "For the Son of Man came to seek and to save what was lost" (Luke 19:10). Jesus loves the lost, the orphans, the lonely, the sinners—even the ones who miss the whole point. That's exactly who he came to save! You and me! The Law-keepers who need his boundless love most desperately. And Edith.

The words to an old hymn I sang as a child still make me teary-eyed. (I heard they were scratched into the wall of some insane asylum. Jesus goes to places like that, too!)

The love of God is greater far
Than tongue or pen can ever tell,
It goes beyond the highest star
And reaches to the lowest hell. . . .

Could we with ink the ocean fill
And were the skies of parchment made,
Were ev'ry stalk on earth a quill
And ev'ry man a scribe by trade,
To write the love of God above
Would drain the ocean dry,
Nor could the scroll contain the whole
Tho' stretched from sky to sky.
How boundless is his love for us! How deep . . . how wide.

Riches take wing, comforts vanish, hope withers, but God's love stays with us . . . forever.

You've Got Mail

~ Patsy Clairmont

When I was a child, I loved to watch my mamaw (grandmother) pull out bundles of letters tied together with yarn from her trunk that sat at the end of her bed. Also inside the trunk were photographs, crocheted potholders she gave as gifts, assorted small treasures, and handmade quilts used to warm up winter. But she valued the letters most, for these were words from those whom she loved. And she carefully read and reread them until they were imprinted on her heart.

Letters bring people near—even if they are on the other side of the world, in the midst of a war, or long past the edges of this finite earth. I've been reading Winston and Clementine Churchill's letters, including wartime notes, which they wrote to each other over a period of fifty-six years. Their correspondence was full of tension and tenderness as they shared their greatest fears and their deepest love. I was impressed with the frequency of their exchanges, many times daily.

Winston and Clementine obviously were devoted to each other, yet the letters also contain some heated moments. Whew, what a relief! When others share their human frailty we're encouraged that we're not the only ones who struggle in relationships.

The record of the Churchills' struggles left clear imprints in their correspondence because the couple wrote letters to each other even when they were sitting in the same room. Clementine realized early on in their relationship that her reactive personality and her tendency to exaggerate to make a point with Winston caused unnecessary strain between them. So, to keep the home atmosphere more cordial and loving and also out of a need to be heard, Clementine would write to Winston about potentially volatile issues, thereby avoiding temperament conflicts. She found that, as she wrote a letter, she remained more objective and less vehement. Therefore, Winston, instead of tuning out his wife, would carefully consider her input. So was born what their daughter called "the house post advocacy," which would not only assist this notable couple in a personal way but would also allow the rest of the world to one day listen in. And so we gain insights into the couple and how they turned communication challenges into memorable communiqués.

Speaking of listening in, I have greatly benefited from the apostle Paul's letters. For instance, when he penned a letter to the new Christians at Philippi, he wrote not from a Hilton suite but from a prison—a dark, dank prison. Not exactly an ideal spot for writing inspirational material, yet he did. In fact, he wrote a joyful message that continues to help millions see what it means to rejoice in all situations. I find it's one thing to tell a person what she *should* do, but quite another to share from what you've *experienced* in your own life. Paul's life was filled with hardships, yet in those difficult places he lived out his faith. And it was during those times that he wrote the rich, directional, foundational letters in what eventually became the New Testament.

As I write to you, there sits on my nightstand a bundle of letters, which includes Paul's, held together by a leather cover. They are love letters written to anyone who has a heart to hear of God's boundless, fearless, stubborn, lavish, outlandish, intentional love. These personal letters have been handed down through the ages, that we might know we aren't alone—not alone in our struggles, not alone in our lives. And the truths in these letters, when written on our hearts, make an eternal difference.

I appreciate that the Scriptures are so full of human frailty while also giving us magnificent glimpses of divinity. That leaves us with hope. Imagine if we allowed the Bible to become our "house post advocacy," that we might read and reread of the Lord's tender feelings for us, that we might allow his words to be imprinted within us, that we might know his boundless love. Surely our own hearts would overflow in response to his.

"Grace to all who love
our Lord Jesus Christ
with an undying love."

—PAUL, IN HIS LETTER
TO THE EPHESIANS (6:24)

"Thou Shalt Not Label"

~ Luci Swindoll

Every morning I eat labeled eggs. Some chicken has written these words on every shell: *Heal Thy Horizons*. What an encouragement to know that when I finish that egg my horizon will be healed—or at least that's the hope of both myself and the chicken.

Marilyn buys the same brand of eggs, and we often ask one another if our horizon was healed that day. It's a fun question with even funnier answers.

Labeling is second nature to me. I do it all the time. It's an easy way to quickly characterize something or someone. For example, I've labeled my CPAP unit, which controls my sleep apnea problems, "Dr. Lecter." The unit has a motor attached to a tube, attached to a mask, attached to my face. Sexy little number! I named it "Dr. Lecter" after the cannibal, Hannibal Lecter, in *Silence of the Lambs*. (Incidentally, I now also travel with a laptop computer I've named "Clarice," the FBI agent in the film.) The gruesome twosome go with me whenever I travel overnight.

But if I'm not careful with this fun labeling thing, I trip myself up. It's not so bad if I'm talking about an object, but when it comes to a person, I can be dead wrong. My label may not even be close to what's actually inside a person. I experienced something several months ago in the grocery store that demonstrates this point (and my periodic smallness of mind).

It was about 9:00 P.M. and I had run down to pick up a few things before bedtime. In the checkout stand I was brought up short by the guy ahead of me; he was covered with tattoos. I mean, literally *covered*. He actually looked more like a rag rug than a human being. His entire body had been scribbled with dark

Crayolas. He was tall with a five-o'clock shadow, looked breath-takingly handsome (what I could see of his face, I mean), and wore only an undershirt and jeans—Pete-Samprass-in-burlap. Immediately I labeled him *Rag Rug Pete*. I figured he must be a hit man or had just finished a bank robbery. It was getting late, and I was sure he'd show up as one of those guys on the late-night news you see in video playbacks, taken during the stickup. But that's not as bad as this: with him he had two children, a tiny baby and a rambunctious toddler.

Rag Rug Pete is a kidnapper, I mused. *He's taken these kids from their mother and he's trying to act cool. Should I report him? Is he going to kill them? Is he going to rob this place? Is he going to kill me?* You know how your mind goes . . . bad to worse, worse to horrible, horrible to death, death to . . . (Well, maybe only my mind goes through these dramatic gymnastics.)

Meanwhile, back at the store . . .

As I was lost in my reverie of judgment, the most interesting thing happened. Rag Rug Pete began to put his groceries on the counter to pay for them (with stolen money?). And it became apparent that the girl sacking his stuff knew him. *Well, of all things!*

"Where's your wife tonight?" she asked.

"Oh, I gave her the night off. I just grabbed the kids and went shopping. She's had to work all day and was dead tired," he said in a deep, warm baritone.

He lifted the baby out of a little bed sitting on the grocery cart and began patting and stroking him in the softest, sweetest way, as he drew the older child to him with a hug. I couldn't believe my eyes.

Then his friend asked, pointing to the kids, "Do you ever leave home without 'em?"

"Rarely," he said. "I don't have enough time with them as it is."

Well. What about that, *Lucille? Were* you *ever wrong—little creep that you are* (accurate label).

You see, I don't like tattoos. They look dirty or sleazy or . . . painful. Something less than "moral." They make me think bad things about people who have them.

Sheila confessed once in a speech that if she ever got a tattoo it would read GOD IS FAITHFUL. Maybe I'd feel okay about that because I know Sheila and I love Sheila and I believe God *is* faithful. But the truth is, I'd have to run it through my personal, preconceived grid that it's okay to have a tattoo in the first place, no matter what it says or is.

By the time Rag Rug Pete left the store, I was hoping he would talk to me, caress me, hold *me* by the hand, and say things like, "If you were mine I'd rarely leave home without you."

So many ordinary people are such angels in disguise. The angel is just hidden under a veneer *we* label "wrong." In his book *Living, Loving, and Learning,* Leo Buscaglia writes, "A loving individual . . . frees himself from labels. You, if you are a loving person, will rule words and not allow words to rule you." That is very good counsel for me, and I would venture to say for all of us.

One of my favorite things about God is that he doesn't get caught up in this labeling stuff. Oh, I'm sure he gets a kick out of some of the wild scenarios I create in my rather twisted imagination. He does have a sense of humor. But he never sticks a one-size-fits-all label on me, or on anyone else. He never just takes one look at a human being and sticks him in a box labeled "good" or "bad" or "hopeless case." No, "The LORD does not look at the things man looks at. Man looks at the outward appearance, but the LORD looks at the heart" (1 Samuel 16:7). God's love is not small-minded or shortsighted like mine sometimes is. His love reaches across all the boundaries human beings try to erect to stay "safe" from one another. In his outrageous grace, he welcomes each one of us to enjoy his boundless love. In his presence we are free of harsh judgments and inaccurate labels.

It isn't easy to break habits that have been part of my life for six decades, but I'm working on it. Every day I'm working on it. God gives me little tests along the way to remind me, "Thou shalt not label." If I can ever get the hang of it, maybe my horizons will be healed.

> This bumper sticker accurately labels almost everyone who drives in front of me: *VISUALIZE* using your turn signals. I had to share that with you . . . in love, of course.

For the Sake of Love

~ Thelma Wells

Y our mother didn't give you away, she just let me keep you for a while."

After a half-century, those words still ring in my mind. What a wise woman my great-grandmother (Granny) was to tell me that over and over until I knew, without a doubt, that my mother had not "given me away" because she didn't love me. She only wanted to make life easier for me than it was for her.

Granny took me in when I was two years old because both my mother and I were ill. Someone needed to nurse me back to health. So Granny did, and my mother was happy and relieved.

One day when I was in elementary school, I remember going to spend the night with my mom. In fact, it is the only time I remember spending the night with her. Maybe I did other times, but if so they didn't have enough significance to remain in my memory. This time did.

My mother and baby sister lived on Starks Street in South Dallas. They lived in a tent. Yes, a camping tent. I had gone camping before during summer retreats with my church, but I had never seen anyone live in a tent day to day. What a shock!

Inside the tent were two cots. Not beds—Army cots (the ugly green kind with the wooden legs that cross and fold like a big purse). Later that night I discovered that my mother slept on one cot and my sister slept on the other. *Where's the bathroom?* I thought. *No bathroom! How will I be able to use the bathroom?* This thought haunted me until the time came and neighbors were kind enough to allow me to use theirs. Inside the tent, there was no stove, just a few sticks on the ground and a big black pot over a wood fire.

My sister and I played until bedtime. *How can both of us sleep on that little cot?* I wondered. I *really* wanted to go home—home to my granny. I was getting very sad. But I didn't want my mother to feel bad, so I didn't say anything.

When we went to bed, I lay very, very still. I was afraid of falling off the cot or pushing my little sister off. The floor was dirt. No rug. No linoleum. Nothing but the hard, earthen floor.

I tried to keep my mother from hearing me cry. As quietly as I could I would sniffle and try to wipe my eyes and nose without drawing attention to myself. All I could think was, *This bed is so gritty. I want to go home where the sheets are white, clean, and pressed. I hate this place. I want to go home so I can eat some good food. I can't stand this place. I want to go home where we have rugs on the floor. I feel so dirty. I want to go home so I can bathe. Why did Granny let me come here? I want to go home!!!*

I don't think my mother slept much that night either. She was a proud lady, and I'm sure she was embarrassed and humiliated about her living conditions. Determined to never ask for a handout, she did what she could to make it in life. Hard times with no work or assistance had driven her to living the best she could, and for a very brief period, that was under the roof of this tent. Because she was crippled in her right hand and foot, my mother had difficulty convincing prospective employers to hire her. While she had more strength in her good left hand than most of us have in both of ours, many people saw only her physical deformities rather than her many abilities and skills.

When morning came, my mother spoke to me in the kindest, sweetest tone. She said, "Thelma, baby, this is no place for you. You need to go home."

That's all I needed to hear! I went to the neighbor's house and asked to use the bathroom again—and the telephone. I called Granny and told her that I needed to come home *now*. She immediately called my grandfather, Daddy Lawrence (her son and my mother's father), to come get me. He came.

Much to his surprise, he saw for the first time how his daughter and granddaughter were living. It broke his heart. He told my mother he would always be there for her. I don't know exactly how things turned around, but I do know that my mother never lived in a tent again. At first, she got a job working for a laundry and cleaning company. Then she worked for Goodwill Industries of Dallas and received awards and commendations for excellence.

As I think back on that experience, I'm reminded of two women in the Bible who were claiming to be the mother of the same boy. (You can read this amazing story in 1 Kings 3:16–28.) In order to settle the dispute, King Solomon told his servants to cut the boy in two and give each woman a half. The real mother of the boy immediately cried in horror, "Please, my lord, give her the living baby! Don't kill him!" (v. 26). Her love for her son was so strong that she would never have allowed him to be destroyed just so she could "keep" him.

I'm sure that's the way my mother felt on that desperate, demoralizing, belittling morning after hearing me quietly sob during the night. She'd rather see me clean, happy, and content with Granny than have me face the ordeals of life like she and my sister were experiencing.

Now that I'm a mother and a grandmother and reflect on that time in my family's life, I don't know if I would have been able to part with either of my children, whatever the circumstances. However, you cannot measure the length someone will go to make things right for the ones they love, including giving them up for the sake of love.

In fact, that's exactly what God did. He gave up his only Son when he sent him down to earth to experience the cruelties and difficulties of life, to literally sacrifice his body in the most humiliating death possible, to give sinners the means to come home and live with him forever. If that's not an outrageous plan to demonstrate his utterly boundless love, I don't know what is.

Few passages in Scripture sum up the glorious love of God and how far he is willing to go for us like Ephesians 3:17–19 (TLB). It is my prayer for you as you bathe in the unfathomable depths of God's love in the pages ahead.

May your roots go down deep into the soil of God's marvelous love; and may you be able to feel and understand, as all God's children should, how long, how wide, how deep, and how high his love really is; and to experience this love for yourselves, though it is so great that you will never see the end of it or fully know or understand it. And so at last you will be filled up with God himself.

Hallelujah!

> A good mother's love for her child is a classic example of Christ's love for us. You will never have a better parent than almighty God!

Fearless
Love

Dear One,

Imagine a former agoraphobic (someone who is housebound with fear) writing to you about fearless love. Why, I can still remember crying out to God for the courage just to drive into town (three miles away), to weather a rainstorm, or to ride in an elevator. But here's the good news: He who is the Fearless One will infuse those of us who are feeling fearful with the stamina, courage, and fortitude necessary to face our daily challenges, whether those be diminutive or daunting.

Actually, few things appear small when viewed through the lens of fear. Fear causes distortions, making enemies giants, trivia titanic, and futures futile. Ask me, I know. Yet I've learned that fearless love not only reduces fear but also rescues us from its joyless clutches.

In the pages ahead, my cohorts on this trek into freedom — Luci, Sheila, Marilyn, Thelma, and Barbara (brave women who have valiantly faced their personal Goliaths) — will wisely and humorously help us press on through the tangle of trials, tragedies, and temptations that clutch at us on this journey called life, leaving us with wobbly knees. Why, these fearless women are even going to let me, the scaredy cat, throw in a word or twenty about my personal grapple with fear and my eventual grip on love — fearless love.

So take our hands and come along. We're on this journey together, and together we'll be reminded of God's perfect love, which casts out every fear.

Holding On,
Patsy

Where He Leads I Will Follow

~ Sheila Walsh

April 2000 was a red-letter month in my household. Barry and I counted off the days on our calendar, eagerly waiting like two homeless people in a soup line. It was the month of "Pat."

Pat Sands came into my life as a knightess on a white horse. I met her in a moment of desperation when I was cohost of *The 700 Club* several years ago. My previous secretary had left just three days before I was going to be out of the office for two weeks on tour with a Christmas musical. I was royally stuck. Who would answer my phones and keep current with my mail, not to mention catch up on the four months' worth of mail my last secretary had left unopened in a box under her desk?

I called a temp agency, and Pat arrived the day before I left. She came into my office to say, "Hi!" Poor woman. My office looked like it had been tended by four two-year-olds. I tried to comfort her. "Look, I don't expect you to even touch that box of old stuff. If you could just answer phones and keep current with what comes in while I'm gone, I'll make sure you receive a Pulitzer prize."

Two weeks later I returned to a huge surprise. Not only was my mail current, but she had also opened, answered, and filed the four-month backlog. I attempted to adopt her, but her children resisted, so I hired her instead. She was not only a wonderful secretary but also a dear friend. When I left the Christian Broadcasting Network, Pat eventually did too, heading back to West Virginia where her grown children and grandchildren live.

As my life as a speaker and writer with Women of Faith became busier and busier, I rehired Pat to help answer mail. She would do it in the evening from her home in Clarksburg. Then I experienced an amazing phenomenon. The gene that was in my first secretary skipped over me and into my husband, Barry. Don't ask me how it happened. They never even met. It's just one of those life mysteries that has no answer here on earth. His idea of filing is to take a large stack of papers and drop them on the carpet, trusting that God will arrange them in the appropriate order on the way down. God seemed resistant. Barry's idea of balancing a checkbook is to see if he can carry it on his head without dropping it. He's good at that. He just doesn't have a clue what all the squiggly writing inside means. He's brilliant at lots of things; he's creative, a marketing genius. But office work? There is no spiritual gift at work there.

So we called Pat. We asked her if she would consider moving to Nashville to run our office. We asked a lot. Pat's husband left her years ago for another woman. He left her to raise four children by herself. Now she was in the same town as them, surrounded by adoring grandchildren. Not only that, but she had just purchased a darling little house and filled it with all her stuff. (Now, as women, we know how important our "stuff" is.) The only cloud on her horizon was a botched kneecap replacement some time back that left her in constant pain. Despite all that, we called her with our gigantic request. (The day that God was handing out the gift of sensitivity, Barry and I were in the rest room.)

Pat's reply was just as I expected: "Let me pray about it. If God says 'Yes!' I'll be there. I'll need to fit in the surgery to redo my kneecap before I leave, but I think I could do that."

I asked her to have her children pray about it too. If I had my mom in the same town as me and someone was attempting to drag her several hundred miles away, I'd be sending a large gift box of Ex-Lax in the mail. Grandmas are not only treasured friends but are built-in trusted baby-sitters too.

Pat called back a few days later. "I'm coming. All my kids feel it's the right thing for me to do. I'd like to come the week after Easter but I can't have my surgery till June, so I guess it'll be July or August."

Barry and I were over the moon! But God had an even bigger surprise in store: a gift for Pat. A gift for a fearless heart that declares, "Where he leads me, I will follow."

It was Sunday night, and Barry, Christian, and I had just returned from a conference in San Jose, California. There was a message to call Pat. "I hope she's okay," I said as I dialed.

"Hey, old buddy. Are you all right?"

"I'm more than all right!" she said.

"Tell me. What happened?"

"I went to a little service in my church. No big names or fancy publicity. I went up for prayer. And, Sheila, God healed my knee!"

"What?" I cried in amazement. (I was also in the rest room when God handed out faith.)

"He healed me. I'm going to go to my doctor and have them do all their tests, but I just know I'm healed."

She went through a barrage of tests, and eventually her doctor wrote on her chart, "Healed by divine intervention."

So, the week after Easter, Pat arrived, and we all celebrated.

One of the many things I love about Pat is the direction of her heart. She's had answered prayers and unanswered prayers. She prayed for months that her husband would come back, and he never did. She has suffered financial hardship and broken dreams. But when it comes to her relationship with God, her answer is always the same words the hymn writer gave us many years ago:

Where he leads I will follow,
Follow all the way.
Follow Jesus ev'ry day.

Someday I want to grow up to have such a fearless love, like Pat's.

God is with you today.
When things work out and when
they don't. In answered prayers
and broken dreams. Will you
follow where he leads?

Unstrung

~ Patsy Clairmont

After my mother-in-law Lena's death, I was given several of her necklaces, including a long strand of pearls. The first time I wore them was on a speaking trip, and as I rushed down the hotel's hall to catch the airport shuttle, the strand broke. I stood helplessly as the pearls bounced away in all directions.

I called to the bellhop, who was twenty steps ahead of me, to wait while I tried to collect them. I had hoped he would help me, but I guess it wasn't in his job description. The pearls weren't expensive, but they were priceless to me because they had belonged to someone I loved. I carefully gathered as many as I could and carried them home in my purse with hopes I could have them restrung.

At one point in my life, I, like Lena's necklace, had frayed until finally my life fell apart. My emotions, like skittish pearls, ricocheted off walls, which left me unstrung. I didn't understand why I was so emotionally frail and fearful or why those around me weren't able to help me gather up my broken parts and put me back together.

But guess what I learned. It wasn't in their job description. It wasn't that they wouldn't; it was that they couldn't. Jesus is the only true Redeemer. He is the only one who can restring my life and yours, who can retrieve all that we've lost, and who can give us back our value.

In the New Testament we have the joy of listening in as the seeking, the lost, the broken, the forgotten, the paralyzed, and the skeptical gather around Jesus. The Lord, who understood their frayed and scattered condition, prescribed truth, direction, wholeness, mercy, forgiveness, love, and liberty for all who came with an ear to hear and a heart to receive.

Interestingly, the ones who were the most receptive were the most obviously damaged (lepers, crippled, grief stricken, neglected). That confirms what I've always suspected: The things we fear (pain, failure, disgrace, rejection, limitations) are ultimately some of our finest teachers, educating us in compassion, grace, wisdom, and understanding.

I have great empathy for those who struggle with erratic emotions because I know how overwhelming unpredictable feelings can be, feelings that flood in with such force they affect even your physical well-being. In my emotionally chaotic years, I had more symptoms than a dog has fleas. But you can treat fleas, whereas neurotic symptoms only leave the doctor scratching his head and the patient feeling hopeless. My fear-based illnesses kept me living a restricted, suffocating lifestyle.

At first, in my agoraphobic years, I coddled my fearful feelings to protect myself. Instead, my indulgence magnified the problem until one day I realized that I had only a few pearls left on my necklace, and I was about to lose those. I was already in relationship with Christ, but if I was to survive, I would have to trust him at new levels. I would have to face my fears.

Slowly, as I inched toward freedom, Christ assisted me in finding my lost and hidden emotions. Pearl by priceless pearl, he restrung my necklace. He taught me to trade in my panic for the pearl of his peace, to switch my weakness for the pearl of his strength, and to exchange my fear for the pearl of his fearlessness.

I love the chorus, "Turn your eyes upon Jesus, look full in his wonderful face, and the things of earth will grow strangely dim in the light of his glory and grace." And that, my friend, includes our fears. They will wither in his presence while we grow in grace.

During my healing trek, I learned I was priceless to him because of his boundless love for me. And that's how he feels about you! So, no matter how unstrung you feel, or how many pearls you've lost, he longs to gather you up in his arms and calm your every fear.

"Errors, like straws,
upon the surface flow;
he who would search for
pearls must dive below."

—JOHN DRYDEN

"I Like That about Him"

~ Marilyn Meberg

Last summer I was with my two grandsons and their mama at a city park. I was swinging two-year-old Alec in my lap, knowing full well I should not be swinging anyone, anywhere, anytime. Swings, cars, planes—almost all motion makes me nauseous. (I am such a travel pleasure.)

The continual back-and-forth motion was getting to me, but I hated to stop simply because of the obvious delight Alec was experiencing: Gamma's lap, a soft breeze in his face, and the security of knowing he could not fall as long as I held him. Little did he know that I was on the verge of losing my grip on him as well as my grip on lunch.

Yielding to the practical concerns about to overwhelm me, I stopped the swing, set Alec on his feet, and attempted to get on my own. As I sank to the grass under a tree, Alec flexed his little knees, peered up into my face, and asked, "You in bad shape, Gamma?"

"I'm not really in bad shape, honey. Gamma just doesn't swing well."

After several moments of reflection Alec asked, "Does you forget how?"

Slightly insulted at his insinuation that age and memory loss had taken their toll, I told him I remembered how to swing but that I really don't like to swing. (It didn't seem prudent to get into the whole nausea topic.) My displeasure with swinging appeared to momentarily mystify Alec, but apparently he came up with an interpretation that was satisfactory. He went over to the slide and announced to big brother Ian that "Gamma 'barrassed."

"Why?" Ian asked.

"Can't swing," Alec replied without compassion.

Ever the sensitive little man, Ian came over and sat beside me on the grass. Taking a different tack than his brother, Ian asked if I was afraid of swinging and was that why I was sitting on the grass. I remembered he was at least eighteen months old before he would even venture near a swing; for some reason he was terrified of them. Assuming I was suffering from his early fears, Ian then asked if I thought Jesus could help me.

That question put me into an immediate theological bind because if I said, yes, Jesus could help me, I would probably need to get back on the swing as evidence of my faith. If I said no, I would be demonstrating limiting God in the small things (like swings) but implying that somehow he helped for the big things like . . . who knows where to draw the line? Is there a line? Mercy!

I came up with what I thought was a brilliant response, which kept me from theological jeopardy. I told Ian, "Jesus is helping me right now . . . this very minute as we sit on the grass."

Ian's little face relaxed and he said, "That's good. . . . I like that about him."

Several months ago Ian, Alec, and their parents (my daughter, Beth, and her husband, Steve) moved to Palm Desert, California, where I live. They are only five minutes from me (eight if I miss the light at the intersection).

Last weekend Ian and I were sitting on my back patio looking out at the golf course and chatting about everything from why his mom should let him swim with or without her in the pool, to why he liked Tootsie Rolls better than suckers. He also wanted me not to worry about his teeth "'cause he was gettin' new ones anyway."

In the midst of this exchange there was sudden frantic chirping and flapping of wings from a nearby bird's nest that I'd observed a week ago. I was especially aware of this nest because I had watched the gardeners pruning the shrub in which the nest was located. They had carefully trimmed the bush, leaving a nonsymmetrical tuft of branches lurching off to the side which ensured the stability of the little hatching house nestled within. What could have appeared as evidence of bad eyesight on behalf of the gardeners was, in reality, sensitivity from their hearts. I had kept an eye on the energetic comings and goings of the little plant tenants ever since the pruning.

What had set the birds off was a poorly hit golf ball that ricocheted off the bush and then skipped into the duck pond a few feet away. Except for a few more bird complaints everyone settled down, including the golfer.

Ian was fascinated by the history of the little bird home and felt bad about their scare from the golf ball. Rising to the possibility of being a grandmother of spiritual influence, I decided to do a little sermonizing. I asked if he remembered talking to me about my supposed fear of swinging and that he'd questioned if I thought maybe Jesus could help me with that fear. He seemed to have no memory of the event, so I skipped to the present and said that Jesus cared if any of us is scared . . . not only grandmas but birds as well. Ian was more interested in returning to the subject of Tootsie Rolls, the swimming pool, and then a new topic: his friend's baby sister. Apparently both Ian and his friend thought the baby was boring. *So much for being a grandmother of spiritual influence,* I thought, as I empathized with Ian that the baby didn't even like trucks.

Several days later I popped in on the kids briefly to say hi and deliver a pocket full of Tootsie Rolls. As I was walking back to my car, Ian ran over to me, grabbed my hand, and said, "Maungya . . . you 'member that about Jesus and the birds at your house?"

"Yes," I said eagerly.

"Well, you know . . . I like that about him."

Moments later, as I sat in my favorite patio chair enjoying the delicious early evening grass smells and, of course, keeping an eye on the bird shrub, I was immersed in the tenderness of God's love. Psalm 50:11 states: "I know every bird of the mountains, and everything that moves in the field is Mine" (NASB).

Watching the busy shrub activity I thought, *They don't even know . . . they haven't a clue that it is God who made them. It is God himself who delights in them and provides for them. They never need to be afraid.*

On the heels of those thoughts came the even sweeter reminder that Jesus expressed in Matthew 6:26: "Look at the birds of the air, that they do not sow, nor reap nor gather into barns, and yet your heavenly Father feeds them. Are you not worth much more than they?"

Ah yes, I thought, sinking more deeply into my chair . . . *I like that about him.*

"Our Father's love is deeper and wilder than we typically imagine."

—DUDLEY J. DELFFS

I like that about him!

The Fetish Priest

~ Thelma Wells

In "One Great Fellowship," Luci told you about the trip we took to Ghana last February to help World Vision meet the needs of the villagers. I had just finished meeting the family I had signed up to sponsor through World Vision when our language interpreter, Cecilia, asked if I wanted to visit the shrine of the fetish priest.

Fetish priest? I wondered with some trepidation. *What's a fetish priest? Is he a devil worshipper? Will he try to harm us?* Internally I asked myself these questions, but I simply replied, "Yes."

My new World Vision "family"—Charles and his wife and three children—are Christians. They believe in the matchless name of Jesus. But Charles's father does not. He is the chief of the village and the priest of the ancestral religion most of the residents practice. They believe that the souls of animals and other ancestral spirits can cast spells or work magic. They sacrifice animals in worship to empower the spirits to help them. In essence, they are idol worshippers.

Cecilia told me that the fetish priest was angry with his son for becoming a Christian and not following their ancestral religion. When Charles found Christ, his father despised him for it, she said. In fact, the villagers think that Charles lost his eyesight over a year ago because his father put a spell on him to make him turn back to his old religion.

As we began our short walk across the red clay dirt to the shrine, I really didn't have any fear. I just prayed in my heart that Jesus' blood would cover us and protect us. When we arrived at the shrine, there were bones, dried blood, a disturbing odor, and other evidences of animal sacrifice. Whew! Fear was all over Cecilia. She was shaking, her voice was trembling, her eyes were wide. Me, I just walked up to the shrine, greeted the priest in the name of Jehovah, our Creator, and Jesus Christ, our Savior. Because protocol is very important to the villagers, I also acknowledged the priest as chief and Charles's father.

Amazingly, I had absolutely no inhibitions as I started telling him that Jesus Christ is the Paschal Lamb who paid the price for human sin on Calvary so that we would never again have to make a blood sacrifice of an animal. I told Charles's father that the thorns that were placed on Jesus' head caused his head to bleed for *him*, the fetish priest. The blood from the nails hammered into Christ's hands was shed for him too. The blood that poured from Jesus' feet when the spikes were driven through was shed for all of us so that we would never again have to depend on the blood of an animal for help.

Cecilia was trembling so bad I wondered if she was really interpreting for him what I was saying. But the priest was definitely listening. I wondered whether he understood English. He seemed to comprehend exactly what I was saying.

I asked the priest what he wanted most in life. He replied, "I want peace. I'm worried about my son who is blind. I cannot sleep at night worrying about him."

Peace. *Isn't that what we all want?* I thought.

I replied, "Peace can be yours right this minute because we have the Peace Maker, Jesus Christ, here with us. He shed his precious blood so you could have peace. If you accept him as your Savior right now, I promise you he will place peace in your heart. You will be able to lie down without worrying about Charles, just as Charles is now able to lie down in peace. I have not seen any greater faith than that of your son and his wife. Will you accept Jesus who promises peace?"

I waited for Cecilia to finish translating what I'd said. The priest just nodded his head but did not indicate acceptance. I offered him a challenge: "If you don't accept today, will you promise me that when Charles regains his sight, this will be a sign to you that Jesus is real and you will accept him then?"

He made the sign of the cross. I interpreted that as "Yes."

In the meantime, Luci had gathered the little children of the village and was teaching them to sing "Jesus Loves Me, This I Know." One of the World Vision workers told Luci that the tree the children were singing under was an evil tree. Steve Arterburn, the CEO of Women of Faith, replied, "They call it evil, but God calls it good."

You see, we were standing in Satan's territory, but *we had no fear.* Our love and trust in God was demonstrated by our stand for him. His love for us was demonstrated by his protection of us. Therefore, we were able to show love for the people and experience the power to represent Christ boldly.

I firmly believe that God is going to restore Charles's sight by either proper medical treatment or a miracle. I firmly believe that God is drawing Charles's father to himself, along with everyone in the Duabone village.

God is so organized. His timing is perfect. That very morning—Friday, February 26, 2000—I wrote this prayer in my journal:

> Lord, today is the day we go into the village and visit our families who are a part of the Family Sponsorship Project. At dinner last night, I accepted the responsibility to care for a family of five with a blind father. Today, Lord, is your day to shine through me. Please, Sir, give me the words to say, the articulation to say them, and the proper interpretation of your Word. Then let your Word be welcomed by the family.
>
> Oh Lord, our Lord, how excellent is your name in all the earth! I honor you with my whole heart. Thank you for this opportunity to serve you in my mother country. Lord, please help me to express how I really feel about this land, this experience, this opportunity, this hope. Let love abound in this place. Lord, please cover me with your blood. Please protect all of us from diseases, lice, bites, food poisoning, water contamination, and all other forms of sickness, hurt, harm, and danger. Father, in the name of Jesus, I denounce witchcraft,

superstition, the occult, divination, libation, animism, and all other gods and demon worship in Jesus' name. I plead the blood in the Name that is above all other names. The matchless blood of Jesus is on us today. Take me out of me and replace me with you. Amen.

God did it! He replaced what could have been a spirit of fear with a heart of love.

You don't have to go to Africa and speak to a fetish priest to need fearless love. You might be going through a scary situation right now, right in your own heart. But God has not given you a spirit of fear, "but of power, and of love, and of a sound mind" (2 Timothy 1:7 KJV). So, recite 1 John 4:18 over and over again: "There is no fear in love. But perfect love drives out fear." And then, my dear sisters, walk boldly forth in fearless love.

When faith is small and hope doubts, love conquers. We never have to live in fear because God's love is perfect!

My Dependable Love

~ Luci Swindoll

here are few words as disturbing as "terrorist," especially when you think you're sitting across the aisle from one.

I had boarded in New York for a flight to Miami and was happily seated in 14F, already into a fascinating book and cup of coffee, when I noticed the dude with the earphones. He was across the aisle, one row ahead, and not only indifferent to the request of the flight attendant to turn down the radio strapped to his waist, but every swig of beer was timed to the drumbeats of the music. His hair was actually blowing away from his face. Whoa!

We taxied back from the gate, and I have to admit everybody nearby began exchanging suspicious glances except the scrawny little dirty guy in 13B who had his eyes closed, feeling no pain. His five-o'clock shadow told me he either got up too late to shave or had blunted his razor while slitting his lover's throat less than an hour before. I chose the latter conclusion.

We were airborne when a second flight attendant tried to coax Harry Dicer into turning down his radio, to no avail. He absolutely refused to obey, so life went on as normal in our little doomed ship of fools. The meal was offered and Harry refused that. He asked for a beer, gulping it as the rest of us ate. He requested a second beer and was given one. Huh? By now the questioning glances had become outright, downright staring.

At this very moment (about forty minutes into the flight), when we were sure our guy was going to pull out a grenade and blow us out of the sky, the head flight attendant, a tall, pretty blond woman with a calm, wide smile, walked up to terrorist Harry and said, "Sir, may I suggest you kindly lower your earphones? I'd like to ask you something."

Disarmed and struck dumb, he actually did so as every book and newspaper for miles around dropped to our laps with a pronounced thud. We watched and listened to this mesmerizing exchange:

"May I offer you something to eat? I realize you've had nothing but beer since you got on the plane. Surely you must be hungry."

"Do we go over water?"

"I beg your pardon?"

"Do we go over water . . . does this plane fly over the water?"

In calm assurance the attendant replied, "Yes, we do. For about 100 miles we are over the outer shoreline of the Atlantic Ocean."

"Are there life preservers on this plane?"

"Yes, they're under each seat." She smiled, looking straight at him.

Of course there are life preservers on this plane, you moron. You would have known that if you'd had the brains and thoughtfulness to lower your idiotic earphones and listen in the first place, but you were too into your beer and stupidity to think of anybody else but yourself . . .

I digress.

"I'd like you to demonstrate one for me," said the terrorist.

At this his new friend asked him to stand, and with the greatest of ease and composure, she took the life jacket from under his seat, pulled it out of its sheath, put it on, and blew it up. All the while she talked with complete coolheadedness, explaining what to do if it was ever needed in an emergency situation.

"Would you like to try it on, sir?" she asked.

(Let me just interject, you could have heard a pin drop on that plane, even over the roar of the engines. All eyes, hearts, minds, and stomachs were riveted on this unequally yoked pair standing in the aisle. I just knew this was truly my final hour.)

Then it happened. The man with the radio, full of beer and bravado, replied, "No, thank you . . . that won't be necessary. I see how it works. I know you won't believe this, but I have never ever flown before. Never been in a plane or near a plane in my life, and

I'm scared to death. I just wanted to know how these things work in case we crash."

WHAT??? Is that it? Is that all??? Good grief, one of your victims would have been glad to hold your hand, you jerk. Why didn't you just say I'M SCARED and act normal like the rest of us?

"I understand," responded our heroine. "Fear is a very natural emotion. A lot of people are afraid to fly. Why don't you gather up your things, come to the back of the plane with me, and we'll visit while you eat dinner?" And off they went.

Although this episode happened about eight years ago, I've never forgotten it. Never will. I know nothing about that flight attendant. I don't even remember her name. But because of her kind, courageous behavior to a rude and defiant individual, she has impressed me for life. I think of her sometimes when I'm facing a scary-looking stranger. She demonstrated fearless love in a precarious situation. She didn't know any more about the man on the plane than we did, but she was in charge, so she took charge. Lovingly.

I believe this is one of the hardest, most challenging ways to express love. It is for me. It calls for courage I just don't have. It's built on an inner strength and boldness that is hidden somewhere inside, coming to the surface only in the most uncommon hour. The testing hour. And here's why it works:

> You've been a safe place for me, a good place to hide.
> Strong God, I'm watching you do it, I can always
>   count on you—
> God, my dependable love.

> —*Psalm 59:16–17 MSG*

That's it . . . those last four words: *God, my dependable love.* You don't have to crank out that kind of love. It's of God. It *is* God. That's why it's fearless.

True courage is cool and calm,
not intense or proud.
It's accepting difficult or
disagreeable facts with
peace and poise.

The Playground of Our Lives

~ Sheila Walsh

It was *that* Sunday again. Barry and I looked at each other.
Was one of us sick perhaps?
Could it be infectious?

Unfortunately, we both looked fine. We'd have to go. I'd received the little reminder postcard in the mail the previous week. They try to make it look fun. Just like the card from the dentist's office that tells you it's been six months since they last scraped the life out of your teeth. Your gums are only now healing. But there it is, an annoyingly happy face with sparkling white teeth saying, *Come on down!*

This one was from our church. It has a perky little jigsaw puzzle on it to remind us that as the body of Christ we all have a part to play to make the picture complete. And it was our turn to work in the church nursery. Thirteen screaming, jumping, fighting three-year-olds—one of them our own.

I fixed a good breakfast—the kind you eat before a marathon race or a military conflict in the Gulf. We took our vitamins. We sprayed fabric guard on our clothes. Chins up, and we were out the door.

We got there early to prepare the room. We read the two sheets of instructions left on the table for us.

Arrive by 8:30. Children will begin arriving at 8:45.
Have the modeling clay on the table ready for the children.
Spread some toys and trucks on the floor.
Take the children for a bathroom break at ten. Change
    diapers of any who still wear them.
Wash their hands before their snack. Each child gets two
    cookies and apple juice. [I noticed that it didn't say how
    many we got.]

If it's a sunny day, feel free to let the children play outside.
  [Please, God!]
Sunday school teacher will arrive at 11:00. Assist her in any
  way you can. [We could leave.]
Parents will collect children before 12:00.
Clean up room.
Thank you for serving God and our church.
Go home and collapse. [I added that.]

They began to pour in. Smiling faces and tear-streaked faces.
Barry attempted to help a boy make a crocodile out of blue Play-
Doh, but the child was unimpressed. I could tell exactly what he was
thinking: *That doesn't look one bit like a crocodile. It looks like a rug with
a tail.*

I held the little girl who wanted her mommy and told her a story
about a cat named Frank who always wore a sock on his head. It
seemed to help a little. She dried her nose on my sweater.

Then Christian ran up to me.

"That boy said 'stupid,' Mommy."

"Well, that was naughty."

"Give him a time out, Mommy."

"But I didn't hear him, darling."

"But I'm telling you!"

"I appreciate that. Why don't we just all go out and play on the
sliding board."

"So, do I get to say 'stupid' now?"

"No."

"Why?"

"Because I said so."

"Well, that's stupid!"

We go out and play. Barry and I look at each other with the
mutual empathy of the condemned. Another class comes out to join
us. They are the "big boys and girls"—four years old. I ask Barry if
he's counted ours. No. We both panic. What if we lose one? I run

back in and count the names on the sign-in sheet. Thirteen. I go back out to the playground and tell Barry that as long as we have thirteen at the end of the day, we're fine. He asks if it matters which ones.

Then I hear that noise that I can hear above a brass band or low-flying jet engines. Christian is crying. I spot him and rush over.

"What's the matter, darling?"

His bottom lip is quivering, and he can't talk for a moment. I pick him up and rock him.

"Those boys said I can't play with them. They said I'm a baby."

Tears streamed down his cheeks, and the look in his eyes was physically painful to me. It's *I don't fit in.* It's *I'm not accepted.* It's *they don't like me.* It's *I'm afraid.*

No matter what our age, we all have those moments, don't we? We all long to be accepted, but so many times we're not. Perhaps that's why we become so defensive, why we allow ourselves to be angry or look tough rather than to feel fear.

One thing I do know to be true: We will never be rejected by God. He will never be too busy for us or annoyed by us. He will never call us names or make us feel small in a way that destroys our dignity. In fact, he hears the smallest whimper we make over the din of the wide, wide world, and he rushes to our side in a heartbeat.

They cried to you and were saved;
in you they trusted and were not disappointed.

—Psalm 22:5

I learn a lot through my little son. When he is hurt, he cries. He tells me what made him sad, and he allows himself to be comforted. God is there for us with open arms if we will be honest enough to present ourselves needy and hurt. He will hear our every cry. He will comfort us, dust us off, kiss away our tears, and send us back—fearless—to the playground of our lives.

When you read about God's love, do you find it easier to believe it's for everyone else but you? It's for you. It's all for you.

The Porn King Who Found God

~ Thelma Wells

I'm like the old lady who lived in the shoe; I have so many children I don't know what to do. But I love them all!

My three natural children have five children of their own. But I also have "spiritually adopted" children who live all over the world—from Hawaii to New York, from Oklahoma to the Bahamas, from Australia to Africa, and other parts in between. Some of them are sick, and I pray for them. Some of them are going through rocky relationships. Many of them need a mentor or just someone to listen to them and help them make wise decisions. Others are just not sure where their niche is in life. I don't have all the answers to their problems, but God does. So I call on him in every situation.

I first met one of my adopted children in the airport in Washington, D.C. I walked off the airplane and heard an excited, boisterous male voice calling, "Thelma Wells! You're Thelma Wells! I would know you anywhere. Do you know who I am? I know this is the Lord's will. I can't believe you're right here at the gate where I'm leaving Washington and you're coming to Washington."

I was somewhat startled. He looked familiar, but I wasn't sure who he was. Then I remembered: I had seen his picture in the March 2000 issue of *Charisma and Christian Life Magazine*. He was featured in an article written by Andy Butcher entitled "How a Porn King Found God." He was Steve Lane, and he proudly proclaimed, "I'm the porn king who found God."

He quickly told me his story. "Thelma, God delivered me and my brother from pornography, and now I'm free to warn the world that pornography destroys. I want you to help me. Meeting like this is not a coincidence. I need to talk with you. How soon can we talk?"

We agreed to talk in a few weeks since I was on my way out of the country. At first, we communicated by e-mail; then one morning he called.

"Hey, Thelma, do you know who this is? This is Steve Lane. I'm so glad we met in Washington. My mother died when I was seventeen years old. I've needed a mother all these years. Will you please be my mother?"

I chuckled and assured him I'd be proud to be the "mother" of a fearless, sold-out, blood-washed, handsome, charismatic young soldier of the cross who's bold enough to give up millions of dollars for the cause of Christ.

Then he asked me if I would be ashamed to tell people I was his mother because I'm black and he's white. I replied, "Heck, naw! I love you no matter what you've done or what color you are—red, yellow, black, or white. All of us are precious in God's sight."

He agreed. "Thelma, I've learned that whatever we do, wherever we go, whoever we attempt to become, there is nowhere to run from God. He simply loves us too much to leave us to ourselves and our own foolish schemes."

The conversation continued with laughter and promises and prayer. I discovered that this young man has a fearless love for God that is empowering him to be aggressive for the gospel even in the midst of criticism.

Steve was raised in the church and had given his life to Christ at an early age. But he saw the hypocrisy of many Christians. He became disenchanted and, in rebellion, became one of the biggest opponents of the church. He produced hard-core pornographic magazines and Web sites for two years. Then, in 1998, God tracked him down and reminded him who he was: a precious child of the King! Steve rededicated himself to Christ and committed his life to warning others about the destructive power of pornography. He now proclaims, "All the garbage in my brain has been washed away by the blood of the Lamb!"

Steve knows, as many of us do, that whatever we do, wherever we go, whoever we pretend to be, God knows our address and has our business card. Just like he caught up with Steve, he will catch up with you. You can run behind money, fame, prestige, filth, shame, blame, lies . . . but there's really no place to hide. King David realized this awesome truth.

> Where can I go from your Spirit?
> Where can I flee from your presence?
> If I go up to the heavens, you are there;
> if I make my bed in the depths, you are there.
> If I rise on the wings of the dawn,
> if I settle on the far side of the sea,
> even there your hand will guide me,
> your right hand will hold me fast.
>
> —*Psalm 139:7–10*

You see, Jesus loves you passionately, tenaciously, unconditionally. He doesn't depend on e-mail or the telephone to communicate with you. He is never out of the country when you call. He is closer than the air you breathe. If you are running from God because of your past or present lifestyle, he invites you to let him give you peace and rest. He will never leave you or forsake you, because his perfect love is fearless. There is nowhere he's afraid to go, no part of you he's afraid to face.

Steve Lane may be referred to as "the porn king who found God," but the truth is, he's just another lost child found by the God who pursues those he loves to the ends of the earth. Will you let him find you?

Come out, come out, wherever you are! Even in our unrighteousness, Jesus loves us — every one.

Resign or Rejoice

~ Marilyn Meberg

Last week my grandson Ian, who will be five years old next month, asked his mother how to keep the devil out of their house. My daughter Beth calmly responded that the best way to keep the devil out of one's house is to have Jesus in one's heart. She explained how that could happen. Ian eagerly prayed a prayer inviting Jesus in and the devil out.

Though I was thrilled to hear of Ian's prayer, I was troubled by the fears that prompted his decision. What had he heard or imagined or even experienced that gave rise to his fears? Ian's family environment is free of many of the "survival" needs common to some children's households, but nonetheless he was not feeling entirely safe.

Ian asked me yesterday if I ever watched Mr. Rogers. I told him I used to watch him with Beth. That information seemed to be more than he could sort out. Finally, he said softly, "Mr. Rogers is nice."

The longevity of the highly respected Mr. Rogers television show gives testimony to the need of children to experience an environment of calm assurance and soothing love. For decades Mr. Rogers has somehow managed to make the confusing complexities of life less threatening to children through singing songs and telling stories. With those songs and stories, children settle into an interior place where the prospect of love and security does not seem so improbable.

Recently I read some anonymous person's declaration to "resign" from adulthood and return to the magical, playful, "simple" world of an eight-year-old. "I want to make angels in the snow," he wrote. (Me, too!) "I want to lie under a big oak tree and run a lemonade stand with my friends on a hot summer's day. I want to return to a time when life was simple . . . and all you knew was to be happy because you were blissfully unaware of all the things that should make you worried or upset."

As I reflected on Ian's feelings about the devil and Mr. Rogers, I meandered down memory lane where so many of my own childhood insecurities first showed up. Like my dismal failure with a lemonade stand. Bobby Amdigger and I entered into this business venture with only two lemons between us. He said it didn't matter how many lemons we had as long as we threw lots of sugar and water into the jug. Apparently that was not a recipe favored by the local citizens.

Speaking of dismal failures, the memory of my third-grade math teacher standing beside my desk tapping it rhythmically with her ruler, saying repeatedly, "Think . . . think . . . think . . . " still makes me desperate for recess.

Then there was my fifth-grade tension over Marty Manson and if he liked me better than Dorothea Hootenpile. She was an adorable little girl whom all the boys liked. I was sure I saw a glow in Marty's eye when he looked at her, but he told me I would always be his best girlfriend because I could run faster than anyone in the school. Somehow that didn't give me sufficient confidence; I would rather have been cute and slow than skinny and fast.

When I first read that "resignation" piece I was charmed by the nostalgia of lying under big trees, making angels in the snow, and even the memory of my trying to bring order and sense and "success" to my little world as a child. But now I wonder . . . Was there really such a time or place when innocence and simplicity existed to the exclusion of harsher realities? In other words, is life really "simple" at any age? I think sometimes we so long for what we've never known in this imperfect world that we gloss our history until we're convinced we did know it at one time, and if only we could return to it, all would be well. "The good ol' days" are often just a fabrication based on wishful thinking.

Dwight D. Eisenhower, our thirty-fourth president, said in reference to his childhood, "Our pleasures were simple—they included survival." In a similar vein, George F. Will stated, "Childhood is frequently a solemn business for those inside it."

Yes, Mr. Rogers is nice, the devil's bad, ice cream's good, and broccoli's too green. Childhood events can be wonderful . . . and sometimes brutal. Adulthood is not that different. The bottom-line truth we all know is that we can't really resign from any phase of life.

But I don't think that's bad news. Because our future is utterly secure through Christ's sacrifice for our sins, we need not spend our adult lives longing for what we may or may not have had in terms of "perfection" and simplicity. We will experience all of that in eternity where there is no nostalgic past or wishful future. When we reach our ultimate destination, with Christ in heaven, all time will be present tense; we'll live in a never-ending state of bliss that cannot be improved upon.

But what about the here and now? Are there no pleasures here, no rich and memorable moments? Of course there are! God loves us so lavishly and outlandishly that our blessings in life are too numerous to count—if we have eyes to see. But no human being, be she eight or eighty, has only good days. Returning to a "blissfully unaware" childlike state is not only impossible, but I think the longing itself is only a remnant of the righteous hunger for perfection that God planted in our eternity-bound souls. The good news is that the most incredible best that is yet to come is beyond even our incredible imagination!

In the meantime, I avoid old lemonade recipes, ruler-tapping authority figures, and men who won't admit they prefer women who are cute and slow. I move instead toward people with positive attitudes who realize that no matter where the devil is at the moment, Jesus is everywhere all the time. Because the God in us is so much greater than any evil, sadness, failure, or fear in this world (1 John

4:4), you and I and little Ian can step up to whatever life holds with faith and boldness. God's love is big and strong enough to contain big people and small people at every stage of life. We don't have to resign.

"For God hath not given us the spirit of fear; but of power, and of love, and of a sound mind" (2 Timothy 1:7 KJV). That truth encourages me to rejoice instead of resign!

The Great Expanse

~ Patsy Clairmont

As a child, I required assistance to grab the monkey bars. (Actually, I still need help to reach them.) An adult would lift me up, while my tummy did flip-flops, until I had a firm grip. Then I was released and had to support my own weight. With hand over fist, hand over fist, I would attempt to make my grueling way from rung to rung across the great expanse. But almost always the pull of my weight would be too much, fear would mount as my fingers slipped, and soon I would topple to the ground.

In the same way, sometimes my grip on God's love slips. That's when I need his help to find my way home, across the great expanse.

God's fearless love not only assists us but also catches us when we fall. Fearless love is sensitive to the truth that we are too little for high things. Fearless love will support us in our efforts to reach beyond ourselves. And fearless love will steady us until we reach the safety of the other side. I like that . . . a lot.

I'm not sure if my humanity or my insecurity is responsible, but I'm given to the misconception that, when I slip and mess up, I must earn my way back into God's good graces. *Surely the process of reconciliation couldn't be as simple as regret and confession,* I tell myself. My sins seem inexcusable, especially considering how long I've known the Lord.

I'm grateful I'm not God. His heart, unlike mine, isn't narrow. Only his path is. And it's a slim strip because he knows we need boundaries to keep us from losing our way.

Aging Miriam, Moses' sister and a leader to the wandering Hebrews, stepped outside the boundaries by usurping God's authority. So she was struck with leprosy and cast out of the camp. There Miriam, the once revered leader, sat with a withered body, calling out, "Unclean, unclean!" when anyone approached her. She had lost her grip; the weightiness of her sin had pulled her down.

The angst of Miriam's heart, the humiliation of her circumstances, must have flooded her with fear. Separated from everything and everyone she loved, Miriam huddled in her personal agony.

My heart aches when I read of Miriam, for I know what it's like to be "unclean" from my sins and to feel like an outcast. I find it frightening to be alone with myself and to face my leprous condition. But I've learned that humiliation often leads to reconciliation, for, as Madeleine L'Engle says, "I know that when I am most monstrous, I am most in need of love." When we get to the end of ourselves, behold: there, at the threshold of change, is God's love that has no fear of the leper in us.

In both Miriam's story and mine we experienced an invitation back into the camp. The Lord longs for our return. Miriam's invitation was sent via the honored prayers of her brothers, Moses and Aaron. To his credit, Moses, who could have been offended, prayed for his offender. We should be so big.

The Scriptures act as a map to help us journey across the great expanse from enemy territory to the safety of the Promised Land. Along the way, we observe the Israelites, who lost their grip and regained it, and we find hope and insight. And while Scripture serves as a life-map for us, God's fearless love acts as a safety net to catch us and then to infuse us with the courage to try again and again and again . . . until we finally reach the other side. Whew!

"I don't know what the future may hold, but I know who holds the future."

—ROBERT ABERNATHY

Damaged in Transit . . .
But Deliverable

~ Barbara Johnson

A package arrived for me today. Or something that resembled a package. The string was hanging off of it, the label was torn, the innards were bulging out of one ripped-up corner. In short, it looked like an elephant had done a toe-dance on my package and then shoved it through the mail slot.

But what was even more intriguing (or irritating) to me was that on top of the package was a stamp from the postal service that boldly proclaimed DAMAGED IN TRANSIT, BUT DELIVERABLE. I thought it was pretty nervy of some postal clerk to call that pack of string and lumps deliverable! Rather indignantly I asked the delivery guy, "Who says this carton should be marked thusly?" He just stared at me like I was the damaged one.

Later I thought, *How many lives, like mine, are damaged and hurt?* We should be marked, "FRAGILE, HANDLE WITH CARE," yet we are all like packages on a long, hard journey. We have been crushed in the vice grip of personal pain; we have been slammed from every side and become unraveled, unglued, undone, and torn apart at the corners. Instead of being treated like fine china, we have been toe-danced on by a whole herd of elephants!

Recently I spoke to a women's group and one darling gal came up to say, "I loved hearing you because you aren't wrapped too tight!" For a moment I didn't know whether to be offended or charmed. Did she think I was coming apart like a ball of yarn? (I didn't realize it was showing this much.) But then I decided she meant it as a compliment. Think about it: not wrapped too tight . . . not so self-protected by heavy packing tape that my life is impenetrable . . . not so "fine" and delicate that I can't survive this clumsy, dangerous world.

And I'm glad. Because I have indeed been on a long, hard journey . . . shoved against the walls of frustration and despair, handled carelessly with no regard for the fragile heart inside, which is already bleeding and broken. But you know, even though I may be "damaged in transit," I'm "deliverable"! But I am on that long trip whose destination is Glory—eternal rejoicing around the throne of God.

Life can be scary, no question about it. I have had some very dark and frightening days, and I'm sure you have too. As someone has said, it sure would be nice if our lives were like VCRs . . . then we could just fast-forward through the crummy times. But there's a wonderful truth that can sustain us as we move forward on this wild ride: we will be claimed by the Master at the end of our trip! Our label may be torn off, our stuffing may be half hanging out, we may even look completely unraveled. But God always recognizes what belongs to him.

> But now, this is what the LORD says—
> he who created you, O Jacob,
> he who formed you, O Israel:
> "Fear not, for I have redeemed you;
> I have summoned you by name; you are mine."
>
> —Isaiah 43:1

We are *his*. What sweet comfort. And we are his at the highest price ever paid: the precious blood of his own Son. "Do you not know that your body is a temple of the Holy Spirit, who is in you, whom you have received from God? You are not your own; you were bought at a price" (1 Corinthians 6:19–20). Because of his fearless love—the love that faced Calvary with no looking back—we, like Christ before us, will ultimately withstand the shocks of life, and our Father will claim his prize. *That's us!*

So, dear friend, if you are feeling slammed, crushed, broken, undone, unraveled, ripped beyond the point of human endurance . . .

remember that God's mark on you is bold and sure. You may be "damaged goods," but you are *deliverable*. Straight into his open arms. You *will* reach your final destination and be ushered into the presence of the Lord who is eagerly waiting to claim you as his own, once and for all. There is no unclaimed freight in God's kingdom.

God's promises are like life preservers. They keep our souls from sinking in a sea of trouble.

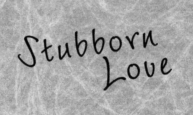

Stubborn
Love

Dear Friends,

A mother of a large number of children was asked by a newspaper reporter, "Which one of your children do you love the most?"

Her reply indicated what a wise and loving parent she is. "I love the one most who is away from home until he returns . . . the one who is sick until she is well . . . the one who is hurt until the hurt disappears . . . the one who is lost until he is found."

God, our Father, through his Son, Jesus, loves each one of us with a fierce longing for our fellowship, an active care for our human frailties, a compassionate tenderness for our hurts, and a joyous embrace for our wandering hearts. Scripture tells us, "When he saw the crowds, he had compassion on them, because they were harassed and helpless, like sheep without a shepherd" (Matthew 9:36). And Jesus himself assures us, "I am the good shepherd; I know my sheep and my sheep know me — just as the Father knows me and I know the Father — and I lay down my life for the sheep" (John 10:14—15).

So, my dear fellow "sheep," rejoice! No matter where you are, no matter how far or hurt or lost, our Good Shepherd loves you with a steadfast, active, stubborn love that will not rest until you are home, well, healed, and found. Come with me and my sheepish friends — Marilyn, Sheila, Thelma, Luci, and Patsy — as we celebrate the stubborn love of our tenderhearted Shepherd.

Love,
Barbara

How Do You Spell Love?

~ Luci Swindoll

I heard a little story recently that brought me pause. When a woman arrived at heaven's gates after succumbing to a long illness, she peeked in and saw people she'd known on earth seated at a beautiful banquet table, enjoying a sumptuous meal. She was amazed and thrilled.

Saint Peter showed up to greet her. "We've been waiting for you," he said. "It's good to see you."

"Thank you!" the woman replied. "How do I get into that banquet? It looks wonderful. I'd love to be with my old friends."

Saint Peter told her that she would have to spell a word correctly.

Having been a spelling bee winner as a child, she felt pretty confident when she asked, "Which word?"

"Love," Saint Peter replied.

She correctly spelled the simple word and was ushered right into the banquet hall.

About six months later Saint Peter asked the woman to mind the store while he ran an errand. During this time her husband arrived at the pearly gates.

"Well, I'm surprised to see you," the woman said, smiling. "How have you been since I died?"

"Oh, I've been great," he enthused. He recounted how he'd married the beautiful young nurse who took care of his wife when she was sick. He'd won the lottery, sold the little house they'd lived in all their married life, and bought a big mansion across town. He bought a brand new Cadillac and traveled around the world with his new wife. Unfortunately, all the fun was cut short by the water ski that plunked him in the head that afternoon while he was vacationing in the Bahamas.

"So, here I am," he said. "How do I get in there? The food looks great!"

"You have to spell a word," his old wife replied.

"Which word?"

"Czechoslovakia."

Consider this silly little story for a minute because there's a very important lesson to be learned. It's awfully hard not to retaliate when we've been hurt or rejected or maligned, isn't it? Wanting to get even is one of the worst battles we all fight. Many people sit around obsessing about ways to get back at somebody. They *love* to get even. But how can the desire to *love* and *get even* live in the same heart at the same moment? It's an oxymoron.

We all know the thought of getting even isn't new. Two thousand years before the birth of Christ the prophet Jeremiah said, "The heart is deceitful above all things and beyond cure. Who can understand it?" (Jeremiah 17:9). The heart will always have the capacity for leaning in an evil direction, even after we have embraced Christ as our Savior and Lord.

So it's certainly a good thing that our entrance into heaven isn't dependent on the correct spelling of a word! Even the word *love*, since no human being can ever live that one out right. Getting into heaven isn't dependent on our doing *anything* correctly, praise God! Redemption rests on the finished work of Christ on the cross.

When Jesus died, he did so for you and me and our "deceitful" hearts that can never get it right. The Bible says the penalty for not getting it right according to God's perfect standard is death, and Christ paid that penalty *for us*. The other great news is that as a result of his Spirit dwelling in us through salvation, we experience divine power to live a life that is above getting even, demanding our "rights," and hurting other people. Christ's death and resurrection empower us to do what we can't muster up in ourselves. Christ sees to it that we can enjoy a love relationship with him today and for all eternity. We can get into heaven with no spelling bee—no contest!

Unfortunately, this does not mean our lives on earth will be easy and without self-centered feelings and desires. As the apostle Paul so clearly states, there is still a natural desire in us to do what is wrong. "I know that nothing good lives in me, that is, in my sinful nature. For I have the desire to do what is good, but I cannot carry it out. For what I do is not the good I want to do; no, the evil I do not want to do—this I keep on doing" (Romans 7:18–19).

How frustrating! As long as we're alive, that tension is not going to go away. But let me suggest a couple of practical things that help me cope with my own desires to do wrong or "get even" at the expense of someone I'm called to love. When I'm able to do this, it really works:

Keep your mouth closed. Every time you want to gossip or speak evil of someone or set the record straight because you've been wronged, stuff a sock in your mouth if you have to. Vengeance belongs to the Lord, and he is fighting for you. Leave the battle to him.

Keep your sin confessed. When sin comes in (and it will), or when you want to get even (and you will), immediately confess that to God. He loves you with a stubborn love that never gives up on you, and he promises to help you in your areas of weakness. The power to overcome is in him, not in you.

Unlike our human love that often goes off course, digging in its heels in righteous indignation, the love of God is righteously stubborn. He didn't die for us for nothing. It was the mercy of the Father that sent the Son to die. Now that's an oxymoron you can sink your teeth into. It's the very essence of how love is correctly spelled.

"Love is an act of forgiveness
in which evil is converted
to good and destruction
into creation."

—HENRI NOUWEN

Greyfriars Bobby

~ Sheila Walsh

It was the middle of the nineteenth century. Queen Victoria was on the throne in London. To the north, many of the people in Scotland struggled to provide for their families. Those who lived off the land were perhaps the hardest hit of all. Bad weather, storms, and floods ruined crops and left entire families penniless and homeless, so they came to the larger cities looking for work.

One such man was John Gray. He arrived in Edinburgh in 1853 with his wife and only son. The situation there was no better. He became only one of many voices crying out for work and a place to sleep. The place he found was cold, damp, and miserable.

One bleak morning in January he got up before dawn, washed his face in cold water, and set off toward the large police station by Saint Giles Cathedral. He was stopped at the door and asked his business.

"I'd like to become a police officer," he said.

"How old are you?"

"I'm forty years of age," he replied.

"We're looking for men half your age, but if the doctor says that you are fit, you will do."

So John Gray became part of the Edinburgh police force. There were two requirements in his new position. One, he had to live in the area of the city that was to be his responsibility, and two, he had to have a watchdog. John found a six-month-old Skye terrier and named him Bobby.

It's hard to think of a Skye terrier as much of a watchdog. Its legs are barely six inches off the ground. It has long, silky hair that hangs over its eyes and a stumpy little tail. But Charles St. John, a famous nature writer in Scotland, wrote that Skye terriers are unusual in many ways. They will lie still for hours at a time. They will eat almost anything given to them. And one of their most peculiar traits, he says, is that they have a tendency to run on three legs as if keeping one on reserve for emergencies!

What John Gray found that day was a true friend for life. Bobby was a fiercely loyal, constant companion on the cold winter nights. Then John's health began to fail. He developed what was common in those days in Scotland: tuberculosis. The only cure was a warm climate or clean air. Edinburgh's air was neither warm nor pure. As a city it was referred to as Old Reekie because of the black soot that bellowed out of the chimney tops.

Bobby sat by his master's bed every day, hoping that he would recover. But in February of 1858, John Gray died. The little dog could not understand why his master was being placed in a wooden box. He followed the coffin to the Greyfriars churchyard and watched as it was placed in a hole in the ground.

John's widow picked up the little dog and took him home. That night Bobby cried and cried by the door until John's son finally let him out. The dog made his way back to Greyfriars Church and to the place where John was buried. He returned there every day. The family tried to make him stay in out of the cold air, but he would cry at the door until someone finally let him out.

John's grave became Bobby's home. He lived fourteen more years. John's widow and son moved on, but Bobby would not leave. There are many reports and photographs in old Scottish newspapers of the little dog whose loyalty and love for his master touched a whole city. If you were to visit Edinburgh today and you made your way to a street called Candlemakers Row, there you would find a statue of Bobby. A monument has been erected to this most unusual dog, now lovingly referred to as Greyfriars Bobby, the terrier who refused to leave his master's grave.

We are moved by this kind of loyalty. We all love to think that we could inspire in man or beast such a fierce devotion. But there is a far greater story than the tale of this dog. It is the story of the total dedication of the heart of God to you and me. If you pick up your Bible and scan the pages of human history, you'll find many common threads. There is the thread of the failure of men and women to live up to their commitments to God, and the failure of God to renege on any of his commitments to them. Such a stubborn love!

> Give thanks to the LORD, for he is good;
> his love endures forever.
> Let the redeemed of the LORD say this—
> those he redeemed from the hand of the foe,
> those he gathered from the lands,
> from east and west, from north and south.
> Some wandered in desert wastelands,
> finding no way to a city where they could settle.
> They were hungry and thirsty, and their lives ebbed away.
> Then they cried out to the LORD in their trouble,
> and he delivered them from their distress.
> He led them by a straight way
> to a city where they could settle.
> Let them give thanks to the LORD for his unfailing love
> and his wonderful deeds for men,
> for he satisfies the thirsty
> and fills the hungry with good things.
>
> —*Psalm 107:1–9*

Six times in that psalm the phrase *unfailing love* is used. This is how God loves us. He will not give up on us or leave our side. When we are strong, he walks with us. When we are weak, he sits with us. On our deathbed he is there to carry us home.

Stubborn love. Resolute, determined, eternal.

No matter where you
are today, you are not alone.
You are surrounded,
undergirded, and guarded by
the unfailing love of God.

Pin the Tale on the Donkey

~ Patsy Clairmont

I know I'm dating myself when I admit that, growing up, I loved to watch Francis the talking mule movies on television. Now, for those youngsters who haven't a clue who Francis is, he was a real mule who starred in several movies. He managed to get into and out of a lot of predicaments but talked only to his master.

Those of you who were Francis fans know the old chap was quite the character and often lived up to his species' reputation of being downright ornery, especially when it worked to his advantage. Francis would at times plop down and refuse to budge, regardless how much others would pull, tug, bribe, or plead.

Which reminds me of another story . . . but this one is a donkey tale, a true saga about a female animal with the gift of gab. What a surprise.

Balaam, an Old Testament prophet, was being enticed by financial gain to call down a curse on the Israelites, God's beloved people. God had a message for Balaam but apparently was having a little problem getting Balaam's attention.

Then one day Balaam mounted his donkey and headed for the plains of Moab when, along the way, the angel of the Lord stood in the path with his sword drawn. The donkey saw the angel and turned off the road, trotting into a field. Balaam, oblivious to the angel's presence, struck the donkey to force her back on the road.

The rider and beast continued their trip when, lo and behold, the angel appeared again. Only this time he stood on a tapered path with walls on both sides. To avoid the angel, the donkey had to press against the wall, scraping Balaam's leg on the rock. Balaam throttled her for this unseemly behavior.

A third time the heavenly visitor blocked a narrow path, which left the donkey no space to pass. So she lay down in the road. Balaam was livid! He took a stick to his stubborn donkey.

Then the most amazing thing happened: the animal spoke. "Hey, you bozo, stop flapping that stick. You know it's not my way to be obstinate. I've carried your carcass faithfully for years, so get off my back." (Okay, so this is my version. Read the real conversation for yourself in Numbers 22.)

Balaam answered the donkey, "You made me look bad in front of my friends. You're lucky I didn't have a sword, or I'd have had donkey burgers for lunch!" (Yes, my version.)

Then the Lord opened Balaam's eyes, and he saw the angel with sword in hand. Balaam bowed down. (Funny how fast we change our stance when the sword is in another's hand.) The angel then informed Balaam that, *thanks to his donkey*, the angel didn't have to kill Balaam.

Wow! Who was the stubborn one? Not the faithful donkey, but the faulty prophet. Balaam had insisted on heading in the wrong direction for the wrong reasons, and a lowly donkey did her best to spare his life. What a picture—a pompous prophet and a divine donkey.

But another picture comes into focus as well. This one is worthy of being enlarged and framed. It's the picture of God's stubborn love for this misguided man. Look at the mercy God showed Balaam over and over again. Why, that angel could have lopped off old Balaam's head with one flick of the sword. He could have skewered Balaam when he was pressed against the wall or parted Balaam's hair clear to his navel when the donkey lay down. But instead God allowed the little servant animal to spare Balaam's life.

While *stubborn* often denotes rebellious resistance like Balaam's insistence to head in the wrong (heart) direction, *stubborn* also exemplifies God's unswerving devotion to his people to help them find their way.

Can you find yourself in this story? Are you Balaam, determined to do your own thing regarding your life direction? Or are you a servant at heart, the kind God allows to see what others miss?

Perhaps, to be on the safe side, you might want to pray this prayer with me: "Lord, if I'm on the wrong road, open my eyes that I might see the truth. May I be wise enough to learn from your servants along the way. And thank you, merciful Father, for your stubborn love. Amen."

"Love is the final end
of the world's history,
the Amen of the universe."

—NOVALIS

An Unbreakable Bond

~ Barbara Johnson

Have you ever gone to the hairdresser and wanted to don a wig or helmet for a few weeks afterward? What is it about a pair of scissors that gives some people an almost sinister thrill as they hold our head in their hands? We come away shorn practically to the scalp, but everyone tries to console us with, "Don't worry, it'll grow out soon!" Some consolation.

Several years ago my sister and brother-in-law were visiting us, and before their departure my sister and I purchased some newfangled hair clippers to give the boys cuts. We persuaded her husband, Mel, to be our first customer. *Heh-heh-heh*. Not knowing how to use the clippers—which came with a little plastic gauge to determine the exact hair length desired—we fit this plastic piece over the clipper and then just sort of *mowed* Mel's hair. Well . . . you can imagine what it looked like.

Since they were leaving the very next day, there was no way to remedy what our little clipper machine had done. Mel's head had furrows plowed on the top and straggly strands on the sides. Fortunately Mel has a good sense of humor. As we waved good-bye to them at the train station, he had a hat pulled *way* down over his head. I called to him cheerily, "Don't worry . . . it'll grow back!"

Oh, if only life itself were so simple. Well, sometimes it is. Our little mistakes and missteps and heartaches can have fairly easy remedies. Time often heals. But then there are the "biggies"—the losses and blunders that cost us dearly. Sometimes what we've lost never "grows back."

I recently read about a pediatric ER doctor in St. Paul, Minnesota, who was being interviewed about his new book, *Julia's Mother: Life Lessons in the Pediatric ER.* Dr. William Bonadio has saved the lives of many children, but, inevitably, seen the lives of others come to a tragic end. And then there are the parents . . .

"When children die," Bonadio says, "they don't die alone. They take something from their parents. Life is changed, after something you held to be truly yours is taken away, is gone; and you realize it can never be the same again. You must start over, but with less, and can never fully believe in anything as being permanently yours."

I don't know where Dr. Bonadio stands on spiritual issues, but his insight into a universal truth is profound: When something we've considered "ours" is taken away, we are faced with the raw reality that nothing in this life really belongs to us. We aren't in control. And change is the name of the game.

I have this wonderful doctor, and some years back I was talking to him about a mutual friend of ours who'd had a face-lift. "Face-lifts are fine," he said, "but they only last for about five years. Nothing is permanent."

"Nothing is permanent." I chewed on that. *True*, I thought. *Nothing this side of heaven is absolute. Nothing is forever. Hair will be shorn; hair will grow back (usually). Faces will fall, no matter how many times we get them lifted. My losses can't be recouped. The future is unknown. Times change, we change, everything changes. Except the taste of postage-stamp glue.*

Just as I was starting to *really* depress myself, another bottom-line truth came into my mind: "I the LORD do not change. So you, O descendants of Jacob, are not destroyed" (Malachi 3:6). Whew! Nothing remains the same (you don't even have to lick postage stamps anymore) . . . *except God.* God's character is immutable and his Word is final. His stubborn love for us never varies or wavers. Regardless of our behavior, our losses, the length of our hair, or the droop of our face, God's promises are true, and his love holds us fast.

Dr. Bonadio's conclusion, after watching life and death, children and parents in the chaotic crucible of emergency rooms over the years, is that there is power in "the only unbreakable bond in this life. And it's absolute between a mother and child."

I would agree that a good mother's love is a powerful thing, but it can't "own" a child or even keep her safe. *Nothing is permanent.* That would be an awfully frightening and defeating conclusion for anyone, mother or not, if there wasn't a P.S. But, thank God, there is! And it is this:

> God is our refuge and strength,
> an ever-present help in trouble.
> Therefore we will not fear, though the earth give way
> and the mountains fall into the heart of the sea,
> though its waters roar and foam
> and the mountains quake with their surging.
> There is a river whose streams make glad the city of God,
> the holy place where the Most High dwells.
> God is within her, she will not fall;
> God will help her at break of day.
> Nations are in uproar, kingdoms fall;
> he lifts his voice, the earth melts.
> The LORD Almighty is with us;
> the God of Jacob is our fortress.

> —*Psalm 46:1–7*

We can never be truly destroyed because our Lord, the Sovereign Ruler of the universe, does not change. He is permanently ours, and we belong to him!

"In order to realize the worth
of the anchor, we need to
feel the stress of the storm."

—CORRIE TEN BOOM

Sheep Tending

~ Thelma Wells

More than thirty years ago, I had the privilege of becoming involved with a ministry that has since served thousands due to the grace of God and the vision of Dr. Robert H. Wilson, Sr. As the pastor at that time of my church, St. John Missionary Baptist, Dr. Wilson founded the Office of Social Services, with the intent of supplying food, clothing, housing, medical assistance, and education to the Oak Cliff neighborhood in Dallas, Texas. When the office opened, Mrs. Edwina Cox Evans became the executive director, and I became a board member.

People with urgent needs began coming from all over the city and county because they could not qualify for assistance anywhere else. There were so many dire needs that in 1976 the Office of Social Services became a nonprofit organization called the Bethlehem Foundation (referred to as the B.F.). This was an appropriate name because Bethlehem means "House of Bread" in Hebrew. Over the years the Bethlehem Foundation grew to include a tutorial program, juvenile prevention and offender program, drug and alcohol treatment counseling center, rent and utility assistance, summer youth program, and AIDS and HIV assistance center.

As a board member alongside the same executive director all these years, I have seen the B.F. thrive in good times and lean times. At times it has struggled as much as the clients it serves. The church still provides some financial assistance, but most of the funds are donations from individual contributions or grants. Financially, thangs ain't been purty a lot of the time. However, in our worst times, the board has always been blown away by the commitment, dedication, creativity, faith, and stubborn love of the executive director.

Mrs. Evans and I can get into some pretty heated arguments about where the next nickel is coming from. To be honest, sometimes she gets on my last nerve. Some of the board members have even thought about closing down. But not Mrs. Evans. More than once she has tearfully, or with fire in her eyes, reminded us, "This is the Lord's program! He put me here to help people. *He* will tell us when it's time to close shop. He is ever aware of our needs, and he has promised to meet them. Don't you know that the cattle on a thousand hills are his? All he has to do is sell one cow! You board members can go your merry way if you want to, but I'm not budging until the Lord says so!"

Mrs. Evans's words challenge the eight of us to keep our focus on the mission Jesus gave Simon Peter in John 21:17, "If you love me, feed my sheep." Mrs. Evans knows that before the gospel will be open-heartedly understood, believed, and received, people's bellies must be full, their bodies clothed, and their shelter provided. She lives by the saying "And they'll know we are Christian by our love." Her love for people extends to putting her personal needs on hold, taking strangers into her home, and counseling many for hours. This love of hers is above and beyond anything I have ever witnessed in my life (and I've been a part of several charitable organizations). There are few boundaries around what Mrs. Evans will do to maintain the integrity of the B.F. and, at the same time, fulfill the needs of people. As a result, thousands upon thousands of people have come to know Jesus Christ as their personal Savior because they've seen his character of love in action.

A few months ago I was sitting in the bathtub, reminiscing. I was reflecting on my fifty-nine years (fifty-five of them as a member of the same church!) and imagining that I was at the judgment seat of Christ. Imagine with me, if you will . . . .

Jesus is looking in the Book of Life. Sure, my name is there. And there are a lot of notations next to it. Yes, I visited prisoners a few times. I was good about sending get-well, sympathy, and birthday cards. I occasionally visited the sick and prayed for them. There were times when I went through my closet and gave away nice clothes and shoes and even shared food from my kitchen cabinets and freezer. Oh, and don't forget the money. God made note of how much money I had given to help the poor. He remembered when I took in a young girl who was a friend of my daughter and kept her for several years through high school and college, treating her like she was my own child.

Jesus went down the list of things I had done. But it concerned me when he asked, "Why, Thelma? Why did you do all this? Was it for me, or for you? Did you do it because you love me and want to be obedient? Did you do it because you love people with the kind of tenacious, unconditional, stubborn love with which I love you every day you draw breath? Or did you do it to impress people and make a name for yourself? Thelma, have you really fed my sheep?"

As I soaked, I thought about a wonderful book I'd read a couple of years before called *This Was Your Life* by Rick Howard and Jamie Lash. The essence of the book is that we who minister must work with a sole purpose in mind: for the glory of God. I encourage you to read 1 Corinthians 3 about what it means to be "God's fellow workers" (v. 9). When we build upon the right foundation, which is Christ and his glory, then once we get to the judgment seat of Christ, when all our works are tried by the fire, they will not be burned up. Instead, we will receive stacks of gold, silver, and precious stones for our service. In short, it's only what we do for Christ that will last forever and "reap the fruit of unfailing love" (Hosea 10:12).

It is certain that what we give to others will come back to us. Isn't that what he promised: what we sow, we will also reap if we do not give up (Galatians 6:7–9)? That's God's faithful, stubborn love in action. The psalmist reflects that our faithful God will never forsake us or leave us begging for bread (Psalm 37:25). In fact, he promises that when we give, we will be given to—in "good measure, pressed down, shaken together and running over" (Luke 6:38).

The love of God is boundless, outlandish, stubborn—like Mrs. Evans's. She has spent most of her life tending God's sheep. What about you?

> "Love is that condition
> in which the happiness of
> another person is essential
> to your own."
>
> —ROBERT HEINLEIN

Tip of the Pencil

~ Marilyn Meberg

Twelve-year-old Boy Stabbed in the Heart by a No. 2 Pencil

How about that for a headline? This bizarre but true story details what happened when a Helena, Montana, boy bounced a football off the wall of his room, dove onto his bed to grab the ball, and somehow drove a pencil through his chest and into his heart.

His mother, responding to his frantic cries for help, dashed to his room and saw the pencil in her son's chest. As a nurse, she knew the worst thing she could do was to yield to the instinct to pull the pencil out of her son's body. To do so would release a torrent of blood, and he could quickly bleed to death. So, with stubborn intensity, she cupped one hand over the pink rubber eraser to prevent her panicked son from yanking it out, and with the other hand she dialed 911.

A CAT scan revealed that the pencil had not only pierced the child's heart, it had penetrated a valve. He would need open-heart surgery, which meant an airlift to the nearest cardiac surgeon and heart-lung machine one hundred miles away.

Three hours later the boy finally made it to the operating table. The doctor put the heart's right side into cardiac arrest, diverted the blood supply to the heart-lung machine, and began repairing the damage. After a successful surgery, the doctor reported that if the pencil had taken a slightly different path into the boy's body, it could have destroyed far more of the heart's blood-pumping machinery. Also, because of the mother's level-headed reaction in not pulling out the pencil, the blood loss was so minimal that the patient needed no transfusion during surgery. Amazingly there was no infection, no contamination from pencil lead, and no permanent heart damage. In less than three weeks, the boy was itching to get back to school.

I've found myself pondering this dramatic story from a number of different angles. For one thing, I'm so impressed by the mother's ability to see beyond the horrific circumstances and do what was best for her child. In her ability to recognize what would be for her son's ultimate good, she fought off the instinct to remove the arrowlike pencil. That firm decision saved his life. At the time it must have made no sense to the child, and in his near hysteria he could well have wondered why his mother seemingly didn't help him. Why did he have to endure such pain and fear? Why the wait? It made no sense. Unlike his mother, the boy didn't see the big picture.

How natural of us all to want an immediate removal of the arrows that pierce our hearts, the pain that consumes our bodies, or the despair that wraps around our souls. We cry out as the psalmist did: "Oh God, do not remain quiet; do not be silent and, Oh God, do not be still" (Psalm 83:1 NASB). In other words, *Do something, and please do it NOW.*

The problem with my desire for a quick fix is that I can miss the big picture of what only God knows is for my better good. That good is frequently accomplished by putting me in waiting mode—and I don't like to wait. I pound on heaven's door sometimes, begging for God to *get on with it*, but God's love is stubborn. It is also merciful. When I must wait, I've experienced the truth of yet another of the psalmist's prayers: "When my anxious thoughts multiply within me, your consolations delight my soul" (Psalm 94:19 NASB).

It is often when I am in deepest need, when my anxiety-riddled thoughts threaten to overwhelm me, that God soothes and consoles me. Those times are the sweetest I have ever known, and yet, even knowing that, I still want the quick fix. However, God knows better what will develop my trust, increase my faith, and enlarge my spiritual understanding. In his perfect love for me, in his stubborn pursuit of my highest good, he says, "Commit everything you do to the LORD. Trust him, and he will help you. . . . Be still in the presence of the LORD, and wait patiently for him to act" (Psalm 37:5, 7 NLT).

In addition to teaching me about his sweet consolations, waiting tests my faith. The truth is, I have no idea how strong my faith is until it's tested. When it is, I am assured it exists; and, in most cases, I am assured I need more faith than I have. But faith is a gift; I can't drum it up or talk myself into it. In my distress I must ask that my faith be increased. Were it not for my need, were it not for the wait, I wouldn't realize I need a faith fix more than a quick fix.

Though most of us want to avoid the pencil arrows that assail us, God, in his sovereign, wise, and stubborn love for us, refuses to rush in and do something that might temporarily relieve our panic . . . but leave us in much worse shape than we already are. Only God has the big picture of who we are becoming and what it will take to make us into his image. During our waiting, he carefully and meticulously performs the heart surgery we need. He knows just when and how to remove that which pierces us so deeply, and he does it without us bleeding to death in spite of what we fear.

Charles H. Spurgeon said: "I willingly bear witness to the fact that I owe more to my Lord's fire, hammer, and file than to anything else in his workshop. Sometimes I wonder if I have ever learned anything except at the end of God's rod. When my classroom is darkest, I see best."

Me too.

Trust that whatever action God is taking — or not taking — in your life right now is for your highest good. God knows what's he's doing.

Abena the Great

~ Luci Swindoll

One of my best-loved places in the world is Africa. As my friend Nicole Johnson says, "It's not just the country, it's everything—the animals, the people, the aliveness I feel. It's connectedness."

Have you ever heard of a little village called Old Kaomkrompe? Well, of course you haven't. Neither had I until three months ago. It's hidden in the Atebubu region of central Ghana . . . way over there in West Africa. But, I'll tell you, it is certainly on the map now and engraved on my heart forever. I have family there.

When World Vision invited the Women of Faith speaking team to visit Ghana, only Thelma and I were able to go. But all six of us sponsored a family as our own to pray for and financially support. Every day now I think of those African siblings and am thrilled to be part of a program that helps enhance the livelihood of family units all over the world.

My particular family's name is Gyambea and the mother, Abena, is truly a phenomenal woman. She's a forty-five-year-old illiterate farmer and the sole supporter of eleven dependents, including seven children, a granddaughter, two nieces, her elderly mother, and a housebound uncle who was paralyzed by a stroke ten years ago. By sponsoring this group of individuals I now have grown from supporting myself, a single person, to the excitement and responsibility of subsidizing twelve others. Overnight I've adopted my own football team, and I *love* it.

Here's why. When I see Abena in my mind's eye, it is hard for me to imagine the stubborn love and devotion that has enabled her to keep her own body and soul together under the most dire circumstances, not to mention those for whom she is responsible. Every day of her life she walks two miles to a small plot of land where she works for six to eight hours, bending over under the boiling sun, planting, weeding, and harvesting crops with two very simple tools—a handmade hoe and a machete. At the end of the day, she heaves a twenty-five-pound bag of yams onto her head and treks back to the village. As the sun sets, she begins the laborious process of peeling, cooking, and pounding the yams into a doughlike paste for the evening meal.

Abena's husband deserted her four years ago after becoming a Muslim and marrying two additional wives. He refuses to provide any financial support for her or their children. The family lives in a small dwelling badly in need of repair. It is made of mud brick and topped with a rusting tin roof. The twelve family members sleep there, cook there, and carry on a daily routine that would put most of us in a Home for Complainers. But not this group.

When I visited the Gyambeas they were all smiles, so very pleasant and kind—eager to welcome us to their home and village. The children were well-behaved and a delight to our hearts. Through an interpreter, Abena told me she sees God's hand in her life. "We have food and a place to live despite my situation. It is only by the grace of God."

Regardless of tremendous hardship, Abena is a cheerful, gentle woman with the most beautiful face and posture I've ever seen. I've decided that carrying large heavy objects on one's head is the secret to standing up straight. I even tried it, but when I almost dropped an evening's meal onto the hard-packed earth, I gave up and sat down. The whole village got a hearty laugh as I determined slumping isn't all that bad.

At the end of our visit Abena told one of the World Vision staff that she had prayed for years that someone would come along to help their family, and she was so glad to have lived to see that happen. I cried. We all cried. That very day we were witnessing an answer to one woman's prayer.

"Abena the Great" I call her . . . the woman with the meager income and the huge heart, the woman with enough stubborn love to hang on when every chip was not only down, but buried in the dirt of an inescapable lifestyle. God made a way for Abena to find hope in the middle of very difficult circumstances, and he does it every day all over the world.

Since our trip to West Africa, Women of Faith, through World Vision, has sponsored one thousand families in Atebubu, and we're branching out to other areas of that great nation. All across America women are becoming financially involved in this wonderful program of love and encouragement. God honors the generosity of his people. We've seen it happen time and time again.

There's a little verse in Isaiah that reads, "I am holding you by your right hand—I, the Lord your God—and I say to you, Don't be afraid; I am here to help you" (Isaiah 41:13). Isn't that a great promise? *I am here to help you.* Abena holds on to her faith, and God helps her. I hold forth in my giving, and God helps me. And best of all, in his loving hand, God holds and helps us both. That's his stubborn love in action.

The day we entered Old Kaomkrompe, we made up a little song: "You can't be grumpy in Old Kaomkrompe. You can't be grumpy in Old Kaomkrompe." We sang it as we laughed our way into that mud-hutted, ramshackle, dirt-covered village of squalor. Little did we know that the people there already passionately lived those words in their hearts.

"Love is a
great beautifier."
—LOUISA MAY ALCOTT

Please Pass the Sandal

~ Marilyn Meberg

A year ago I experienced the most spirit-feeding, soul-enhancing trip of my life. Together with my son, Jeff, his wife, Carla, and my friend Pat, we joined several hundred others for pastor and radio host Chuck Swindoll's tour through Israel.

Quite frankly, I did not anticipate the trip with much excitement. I asked myself why I was going: why spend time and money on something for which I seemed to feel so little enthusiasm? I would answer those ponderings with guilt-laced thoughts like, *Marilyn, as a believer in Christ and student of the Bible, you need to see the places Jesus saw and the sites to which he referred . . . it will broaden your borders and deepen your understandings.* With that bit of moralizing I would try to dismiss the preferences that sent me into reveries of the gentle, sunflower-splashed hills of Tuscany with its luscious food and warm-hearted people. Why wasn't I going there instead, defying death in a rented Fiat instead of nausea in a crowded tour bus?

At that point the most compelling aspect of the trip to the Holy Land was the opportunity to spend two weeks in the company of my son, Jeff, who, in my humble opinion, is the most engagingly fun and gifted young man on the face of the earth!

In spite of my less-than-positive sentiments about the trip, within hours of our arrival in Tel Aviv my entire interior landscape began to change. It was not just that our accommodations, food, and travel companions proved to be fantastic; there was an ever-increasing sense of God-was-here, God-continues-to-be-here, God-will-always-be-here. I'm not suggesting that I have to scout around to find God at home in Palm Desert, California, but there was an almost palpable Presence as we meandered from one biblically significant spot to another. The history of each was richly moving and spiritually rewarding.

As we all sat in the Roman theater in Caesarea, Chuck spoke briefly about covenant and how God has revealed himself as a covenant-making God. To those of us raised in the church, the word *covenant* is not unfamiliar, but I found myself latching onto it with new energy and interest. *Covenant* means "to chain together." It was the highest form of commitment two individuals could share. To covenant with someone was far more serious and binding than to promise.

My imagination was also sparked as I recalled several of the rituals used by people to enter into a covenant. A sword might be passed, signifying that the two would be united as one against the enemy. Or (and I hate this one) they might cut an animal in two and pass between its halves, the symbolism being that as each half, though separated, was still one animal, so the two covenant partners would become as one individual. Far more appealing to me was the ritual of two people passing a sandal between themselves, an action that symbolized they would travel any distance to be at one another's side.

What an incredible covenant God initiated with his creation, I thought as we walked the huge Roman paving stones back to Bus 33. The God of Abraham, Isaac, and Jacob made a covenant with them and their many descendants who followed, saying: "I will live among you. . . . I will walk among you; I will be your God, and you will be my people" (Leviticus 26:11–12 NLT).

And what an equally incredible, blatant disregard his people exhibited toward honoring that covenant! When warned by God about this through Jeremiah the prophet, the Israelites' response was, "Don't waste your breath. We will continue to live as we want to, following our own evil desires" (Jeremiah 18:12 NLT). How could they! How could they refuse the covenant of an as-one relationship with the God of the universe? How stupid! And yet God kept hanging in there with them. Why would he even want to be "as-one" with those fickle people? How, after centuries of their nose-thumbing disobedience, could he say, "I will forgive their wickedness and will remember their sins no more" (Jeremiah 31:34)?

Well, I thought as our tour bus headed out, *covenant or no covenant, I'd have bailed on that bunch. After all, they bailed first.*

Near our tour's conclusion we gathered in the tranquillity and beauty of the grounds at the Garden Tomb located outside the walls of Jerusalem, a place many believe to be the site of the crucifixion and resurrection of Jesus. The lush garden of flowers and low-hanging trees was in stark contrast to the cacophony of sounds bombarding us from every direction: honking horns, bazaar owners yelling descriptions of their wares, grinding transmissions of hundreds of tour buses, as well as the Moslem muezzin calling his people to noontime prayer. Amazingly, in spite of the din beyond the garden walls, divine peace settled over our scene as Chuck led us into the "Remembrance of Me" service. *God was there.*

Aware of his presence and still munching on the word *covenant,* I realized in a fresh way that day that God's covenant with Israel was preparation for the coming of God himself, in the person of his Son, to fulfill all his promises. With the failure of the Israelites to keep his covenant, God showed them the need for a new covenant that would bestow the power to obey.

The power to obey . . . isn't that what we all need? It wasn't just the Israelites who blew it repeatedly and had to be jerk-chained back into line; it's every human being who's ever lived. We lack the power to obey. God knew his standard was humanly impossible, so he made sure we all knew that and then made a new covenant—one that provided for us a perfect person (Jesus) who, through his death on the cross, paid the price for our imperfection (sin). When I enter into that covenant relationship with Christ, I am washed with grace and welcomed as one of his people. My imperfection is forgiven and God forgets it.

Grasping all this and incorporating it consistently will always be a challenge to me, even though Scripture repeatedly tells me I can do nothing in and of myself that will eliminate my bent toward disobedience. Nothing in and of myself will give me the power to obey other than his empowerment.

If I truly believe in the terms of the new covenant, I will recognize that it is the Holy Spirit of God, living in me, who produces that behavior for which I long, but, paradoxically, sometimes fight against. As Paul says, "I realize that I don't have what it takes. I can will it, but I can't *do* it. I decide to do good, but I don't *really* do it. I decide not to do bad, but then I do it anyway. My decisions, such as they are, don't result in actions" (Romans 7:18–20 MSG). The answer to those struggles lies in accepting the terms of the new covenant: Jesus himself living within me, producing that which I can't.

What is behind that huge relief effort is God's love, a stubborn love that will not let me go, a love so tenacious, so gracious, so unfathomable that he willingly made a new covenant with me at the highest price. That covenant is designed to assure me that in spite of poor performance, I am his and he is mine.

My guess is that we all need encouragement to relax in the grace of the new covenant and—ah, yes—to receive the sandal as it is passed.

> "O mad lover! It was
> not enough for you to take
> on our humanity; you had
> to die for us as well."
>
> —CATHERINE OF SIENA

What Would Jesus Do?

~ Thelma Wells

One of the hardest lessons for human beings to learn is that we can't change anybody. We spend much of our lives trying to mold others into our own image. Husbands try to change wives; wives, husbands. Parents attempt to change children; children, parents. Religion hopes to change society; society, religion. It's a futile cycle, but how stubbornly we cling to the belief that we *should* and *can* and *will* succeed!

During the first few years of my marriage, I dedicated myself to changing my husband, George. When I married him, he was perfect. Then, shortly after the honeymoon, he changed! Little things started to annoy me. His grammar wasn't perfect. He was too quiet. He never planned any fun activities for us. In short, he needed help! And as his wife, it was my duty to remake him into a perfect being, according to my own ideals.

Now, when we would discuss *his issues*, he'd reply, "Thelma, this is the way I am and you can't change me. If anyone has changed in this relationship, it's you." Can you believe that? He was accusing *me* of changing! Hmmmph.

As the years ticked by, our idea of the perfect marriage revolved around lifestyle and luxuries. We owned a beautiful home and drove a new car. I shopped at the best department stores and dressed myself as if I had stepped off the pages of *Vogue*. At the age of twenty-five, I was wearing an heirloom diamond ring and a custom-designed mink coat. But I wasn't happy. It wasn't enough. Our marriage needed changing. *George* needed changing.

During that same period, I noticed that our oldest daughter, Vikki, needed changing too. She was a lot like her father—a loner. She would hibernate in front of the television set or hide out in her room and read a book. She was too quiet, especially at times when I needed her to be charming. I would introduce her to people and she would look at them, without smiling or even attempting to look friendly, and mumble a cold, disinterested "Hi." Nothing else, just "Hi."

One day when she was twelve, I introduced her to some church members and she barely spoke. I had had it. When we got in the car, I yelled at her and told her I would no longer tolerate her indifference and "rudeness." I explained what an appropriate greeting was, how embarrassed I was, how impolite she was. On and on I told her about herself, for forty-five loud minutes.

When I finished, she said something I will never forget. With her arms folded in a "get out of my life" posture, she quietly, yet firmly stated, "Mama, I love you. But I'm not you. I don't even want to be like you."

What? You don't want to be like me! Say what? How dare you! You ungrateful little brat! My head was spinning. *What's wrong with me? Why doesn't my own daughter want to be like me? I'm wonderful. Does she not understand that I'm a Proverbs 31 woman?!*

I allowed myself to get so angry with that girl that I didn't even want to feed her, but I had to. She *was* my child. But my feelings were crushed. After all, she came from me. She ought to want to be like me. (Whine-whine.)

But after a few weeks, I understood her statement. What she was really saying was, "Mother, God made me different from you and everybody else. I am a unique person with my own personality, preferences, and desires. Please accept me the way I am and respect my individuality."

What Vikki said as a wise young girl was the catalyst that sparked maturity in me on many levels. I started asking myself why I *needed* to change the people around me. What was wrong with *me* that made it so important for people to act, speak, and portray the image I wanted of them? Why was I so stubborn about having things and people my way?

After much soul searching, I had to admit that the issues I perceived as others' problems were really my own. I observed my own behavior and became consciously aware of my own shortcomings. The change needed to happen in *me*. Ouch.

Once I realized I had been blind to my own faults, I saw just how much love and patience others had with me. During those stormy years of our marriage, my husband never gave up. He loved me with a gracious, unfailing love. He was never angry for an extended length of time. He always tried to reason with me. He made very few demands on me, and he trusted me. My goodness, once I removed the stick out of my own eye, I saw I had me a righteous man!

I'm glad I got over my obsession to change George, Vikki, and others. George and I have been married nearly forty years now, and not only do we love each other, but we like each other too. And Vikki and I are thick as thieves. We are a prime example of how true love can survive turmoil. We have learned that even in the face of adversity, godly love is patient and kind. It is not fault-finding. It is not selfish. It never fails.

Ask yourself this: *Do you really love the people you're trying to change? Can you accept them the way they are? If not, why not? What's it really all about, for you?*

How grateful I've become that God accepts us just exactly as we are. Although he doesn't always condone the way we think, talk, and act, he loves us anyway. He gives us guidelines for proper living and the spiritual power to follow them, but he doesn't force us to do what's right. Through his Word, he shows us, tells us, reminds us again and again how to live. He intends for us to live more abundantly, and he makes it really clear and simple:

> "'Love the Lord your God with all your heart and with all your soul and with all your strength and with all your mind'; and, 'Love your neighbor as yourself.'"   —*Luke 10:27*

So, dear friend, the next time you find yourself trying to change someone, ask yourself, *How would Jesus love this person? What would Jesus do?* You might be amazed at what you discover, not only about how he wants you to love, but also how stubbornly and graciously he loves you!

> When you love the Lord
> with all that is within you,
> and your neighbor as yourself,
> you've covered everything!

"Is That Your Final Answer?"

~ Barbara Johnson

If you've ever watched America's prime-time game show hit *Who Wants to Be a Millionaire?* then you know the white-knuckled suspense that comes with this question from Regis Philbin. *Am I ready to commit to this one, final answer that will either fill my purse with cash or send me off the stage in humiliated defeat?* The contestants act like they have their very souls riding on how they answer each and every question. I don't even like to watch the show; it gives me a stomachache.

Sometimes life seems to be one big long series of questions — sometimes really tough ones that seem to threaten us with disaster if we don't get the answer just "right." We try everything . . . wrack our puny brains . . . use up all the "lifelines" allowed us . . . and sometimes we're still left without solutions to overwhelming problems. Sometimes we don't even know the right *questions*.

"Listen to my prayer, O God," we cry with the psalmist. "Do not ignore my plea; hear me and answer me. My thoughts trouble me and I am distraught" (Psalm 55:1–2). And God does promise to answer us when we call, to tell us "great and unsearchable things" that we do not know (Jeremiah 33:3). It's just that we don't get to dictate when, how, and what he answers. *Rats!* In fact, the writer of Deuteronomy tells us that there are "secret things" that belong only to the Lord (29:29). While he reveals many mysteries to us, and those revelations "belong to us and to our children forever, that we may follow all the words of this law" (Deuteronomy 29:29), he has never promised to give us every answer on demand. There are some things we will have answers to only when we enter his presence in heaven. And then, will we even care? Will it matter?

Innate in the human soul is the deep cry: *Why?* The *whys* we pound on heaven's door with today are echoed down the centuries. "Why is this happening to me?" Rebekah asked the Lord when she became pregnant with twins after years of barrenness (Genesis 25:21–22). "Why have you repaid good with evil?" Joseph demanded to know from his traitorous brothers (Genesis 44:4). "Why is light given to those in misery, and life to the bitter of soul?" Job railed in his anguish (Job 3:20). "My God, my God, why have you forsaken me?" the Son of God cried out in a loud voice as he hung dying on the cross (Matthew 27:46).

Being caught in the web of "why" is an inevitable human experience. We can pray for wisdom and courage to deal with the broken places in our lives; we can work with good counselors who can help us regain our balance in the midst of our private storms; we can hang onto each other for comfort and strength. But ultimately, as we mature in Christ and experience his many answers alongside our many questions, we learn to accept the bottom line: there are secret things that belong to the Lord. We have to learn to trust him for grace to get us through the "answerless" times.

The good news is that our real life is not a game show where the stakes are all or nothing. If we miss some "right" answers along the way, we get our prize anyway! Because of the stubborn love of God that never truly abandons us, even when we hang in torment on our individual crosses, *we are going to be okay*. I know this from personal experience. I know that I am secure because I already have the answer to the million-dollar question!

I love the song that says, "When answers aren't enough, there is Jesus."

Is that your final answer, Barb?

> I pray to you, O LORD,
> in the time of your favor;
> in your great love, O God,
> answer me with your sure salvation.
>
> —*Psalm 69:13*

Yes, that is my final answer.

God believes in you;
therefore, your situation is never
hopeless. God walks with you;
therefore, you are never alone.
God is on your side; therefore,
you can never lose!

Lavish
Love

Ladies,

Jesus loves you so much that he had you on his mind in eternity past, before he even set the stars in place, hung the moon in our galaxy, and made cows and roses. When he called it time for you to be born on earth, he predestined you to be in fellowship with him, to love him and serve him until he takes you back to eternity future to live with him forever. He ordered each one of your days, to give you a hope and a future.

Like a devoted parent, he meets your every need. When you're afraid, he wants to put you at ease. When you're angry, his love soothes. When you're indecisive, he promises to give you wisdom. When you're sorrowful, he longs to comfort you. When you sin, he forgives you and never brings it up again! When you were lost, he sent his only Son to die for you. Early Sunday morning, Jesus rose from the grave — for you. And one of these days, he's coming back for you!

God's love is so sumptuous that he lavishes us with only perfect gifts. His love is so over-the-top that he gives us much more than we deserve. Every day he showers us with love that is purposeful, profuse, extravagant — far beyond anything we can comprehend. Come, now, as Marilyn, Barbara, Luci, Sheila, Patsy, and I celebrate his all-encompassing, enfolding, engaging, enveloping, unfathomable love. Jesus' love just bubbles over in our souls!

Love,
Thelma

Much Ado about Much

~ Patsy Clairmont

My husband, Les, is a lavish kind of guy. If a little works, then he'll do a lot. And if a lot is necessary to fill the bill, then he'll double that. His "giver" is stuck on muchness. Lucky me!

Actually, I've spent a good deal of time trying to temper his extravagant heart—although, just between you and me, I hope I never succeed. I mean, who buys a Ferrari and then has a governor installed? (For those of you who are auto-challenged, a governor is one of those deals they put on cars to keep them from going too fast.) Instead, one looks forward to opening that baby's throttle all the way!

I must say, I find it delightful to unwrap a gift from a lavish giver, to find something inside that takes my breath away. I've also discovered that taking someone who is prone to lavishness with you when you shop for clothes is a good strategy. That way, when you turn boringly practical and decide to settle for less than the best, Mr. Lavish steps in to rescue you. Saleswomen constantly ask me where I found Les since he's always prodding, "Are you only going to buy one outfit? Oh, honey, please get them both."

When our two sons were young, every year at Easter I would send Les scurrying to buy baskets for them. I would carefully instruct him to buy small ones because the kids didn't need a lot of junk food to carve craters in their bicuspids. But every year Mr. Extravagant would come home with some outrageous offering: stuffed rabbits the size of blimps, wagons—yes, wagons—full of candy, grocery sacks bulging with jelly beans, soap bubbles by the jug . . .

I remember one time Les found an unusual teapot he thought I'd enjoy adding to my collection. Then, he decided, if one was great, two would be stupendous. So he bought identical teapots. I thought I was seeing double. This man just doesn't understand moderation.

Moderate means "reasonable, measured, and restrained." It's a wondrous concept, if one is trying to cut costs or lose weight. Yet, even though the principle of moderation fits us like a glove when we speak of food consumption, notice how our interest dwindles when we speak of, say, sky illumination. I mean, imagine if the Lord had been moderate with the stars that he pressed into the velvet night. What if he had tossed out only a handful? Why, we would miss out on the breathtaking moments when we gaze heavenward—not to mention the light source.

Or what if the Lord had become tightfisted when he chiseled the mountains with artistic brilliance? Why, we would have no Grand Canyon, no Swiss Alps, and the Himalayas would be a heap of dust blowing about in the wind.

And what if our only water source was the oceans, but no lakes, streams, or brooks existed? Why, where would we snag a bass, run a stringer of bluegills, or go fly-fishing? And think of all the bare-foot little boys and girls who would miss out on catching pollywogs, turtles, frogs, and snakes. And where would those scalawag fellows take flying, body-smacking leaps into cool ponds on scorching days? Or float their latest hand-carved sailboats?

Here's the best news yet: God wasn't moderate in his love but *lavished* it on us at Calvary. Christ became heaven's door that we might enter in. And we don't have to wait until death to experience heaven's boundless, exquisite love. Christ rescues us daily in myriad ways from settling for less than his dazzling best.

A hymn writer penned it this way: "Heaven came down and glory filled my soul." The risen Christ in us now and through eternity—how lavish can you get?

May showers of blessing
fall lavishly on you today
and fill your soul with glory!

Ooey-Gooey Bible Love

~ Thelma Wells

When I was a teenager, one of the Sunday school teachers in the youth department at our church enticed us to read the juiciest, most sensual love story ever written. He said it was better than any romance novel, and once we started reading it we would not want to put it down. He aroused our curiosity so much that we wanted him to be quiet so we could start reading. Once we started, we discovered he was right: we couldn't put it down.

I had forgotten just how good the story was until my friend Dee told me about her new business in California called Song of Solomon. She customizes engagement, wedding, and anniversary gift baskets using this beautiful love story as the basis for the contents. The baskets contain bath oil, dusting powder, perfume, lingerie, and all sorts of goodies to stimulate a romantic, blissful experience. I had asked her to send baskets to several brides-to-be as shower gifts. All the brides called to rave about the most unusual and perfect gift they'd received. Their response piqued my interest to revisit the spicy book of my youth.

The Song of Solomon (or Song of Songs as it is sometimes called) is a moving, dramatic love story featuring a Jewish maiden and her lover, King Solomon. This dialogue of betrothal, marriage, and sex is placed in the proper perspective—according to God's perfect plan. The beautiful, romantic, sensual, affirming love story is a tale with two meanings. One is the love and affection between the girl and the king; the other is the love and affection between Jesus and his bride—the church.

Do you remember how you felt when you became infatuated with your first love? You know, you wanted to be with him all the

time, talk to him, look deep into his eyes, and hold his hand.
Everything he said was either funny or right. I remember when I fell
in love with my husband, George. I would sit on my front porch and
pray for him to drive by just so I could see him for one second.

When Solomon's beloved recalls their courtship, she reminisces
with these tender words:

> Listen! My lover!
> Look! Here he comes,
> leaping across the mountains,
> bounding over the hills.
> My lover is like a gazelle or a young stag.
> Look! There he stands behind our wall,
> gazing through the windows,
> peering through the lattice.
> My lover spoke and said to me,
> "Arise, my darling,
> my beautiful one, and come with me.
> See! The winter is past;
> the rains are over and gone.
> Flowers appear on the earth;
> the season of singing has come,
> the cooing of doves
> is heard in our land.
> The fig tree forms its early fruit;
> the blossoming vines spread their fragrance.
> Arise, come, my darling;
> my beautiful one, come with me."
>
> *—Song of Songs 2:8–13*

And when they get engaged, King Solomon says to her:

> How beautiful you are, my darling!
> Oh, how beautiful!
> Your eyes behind your veil are doves.

Your hair is like a flock of goats
descending from Mount Gilead.
Your teeth are like a flock of sheep just shorn,
coming up from the washing.
Each has its twin;
not one of them is alone.
Your lips are like a scarlet ribbon;
your mouth is lovely.
Your temples behind your veil
are like the halves of a pomegranate.
Your neck is like the tower of David,
built with elegance;
on it hang a thousand shields,
all of them shields of warriors.
Your two breasts are like two fawns,
like twin fawns of a gazelle
that browse among the lilies.
Until the day breaks
and the shadows flee,
I will go to the mountain of myrrh
and to the hill of incense.
All beautiful you are, my darling;
there is no flaw in you.

—*Song of Songs 4:1–7*

Now if the love between these two isn't lavish, I don't know what is! There are eight chapters in this altogether lovely book of romantic poetry. In chapter eight, the maiden emphasizes that love is as strong as death because it cannot be killed by time or disaster. "Many waters cannot quench love; rivers cannot wash it away" (Song of Songs 8:7). It cannot be bought with a price because it is freely given. It must be accepted as a gift from God and then shared within the guidelines God provides.

I encourage you to get yourself a cup of tea, curl up in your favorite chair, and read this wonderful story about the love of one girl and one king and how their love illustrates God's boundless, fearless, stubborn, lavish, outlandish, intentional love for you. God's love is sweeter than honey dripping from a honeycomb, more beautiful than the first flowers in spring, cozier than a warm blanket on a winter night, peaceful as the gentlest breeze, vast as the full moon surrounded by the endless galaxies, comfortable as a good night's rest.

> And now these three remain: faith, hope and love. But the greatest of these is love. —*1 Corinthians 13:13*

How much more lavish can love get!

Lonely? Longing to be swept off your feet? Fall madly in love with the Lover of your soul — Jesus!

More Than Enough

~ Barbara Johnson

Have you heard the story of the old woman whose life had been a constant struggle against poverty, and who had never seen the ocean? On being taken to the seaside for the first time, she exclaimed, "Thank God there's something there's enough of!"

During times when our cupboards are bare, our hearts are barren, or our souls are parched, it's easy to slip into "deprivation mode." *I'll never have enough*, we worry and whine. *I'll never see "the goodness of the LORD in the land of the living" (Psalm 27:13). God just doesn't care. Or maybe it's just that* I'm *not "enough." Maybe he's depriving me of what I want because I just don't deserve it.* Whine, whine.

Genesis 29–35 tells of the adventure and exhilaration, the traumas and trials of two of Scripture's most colorful characters: Jacob and Rachel. Jacob waited many years to win his beloved Rachel as his wife, "but they seemed like only a few days to him because of his love for her" (29:20). The consummation of their marriage, however, produced no children, and Rachel became frightened that her barrenness would cost her her husband's devoted love. Since God was clearly not paying attention to the deepest desires of her heart, she got desperate and took matters into her own hands. Rather than having her first son according to God's timetable, she insisted that Jacob father a child for her through her servant, Bilhah.

Now, if we tried to pull off a scheme like that today we'd probably get arrested. But haven't we tried, in our own more subtle ways, to win the hearts of people and God alike through all kinds of shenanigans? Fearful that there won't be "enough" to go around, we've strived and connived and tried to be "good enough" to secure our place in the life of someone we love—or even in the kingdom of God.

But it just doesn't work that way. Rachel's attempts to earn the unearnable reflect our own misguided efforts to win what is already ours—and that only through grace. We can't *make* someone love us; we don't need to *win* God's love. And how sad for us when we try. Rachel already had Jacob's whole heart; she just couldn't believe it. And we already have God's whole heart; we just need to trust in that glorious truth.

How? By deciding to take him at his Word.

> Therefore, since we have been justified through faith, we have peace with God through our Lord Jesus Christ, through whom we have gained access by faith into this grace in which we now stand. And we rejoice in the hope of the glory of God. Not only so, but we also rejoice in our sufferings, because we know that suffering produces perseverance; perseverance, character; and character, hope. And hope does not disappoint us, because God has poured out his love into our hearts by the Holy Spirit, whom he has given us. You see, at just the right time, when we were still powerless, Christ died for the ungodly.
> —*Romans 5:1–6*

Scripture is one long, beautiful story of God's patient, perfect, lavish love for humankind. And it's not just a fairy tale! Christ bled and died and rose again so that we could *know*, beyond a shadow of a doubt, that God loves us! Sometimes his love doesn't look the way we want it to at the moment; sometimes we have to wait for answers to our prayers. But his grace is ever-present and his love is never-ending.

It's been said that the Christian life is like the dial of a clock. The hands are God's hands, passing over and over again . . . the short hand of discipline and long hand of mercy. Slowly and surely the hand of discipline must pass, and God speaks at each stroke. But over and over passes the hand of mercy, showering down a twelve-fold blessing for each stroke of heartache and trial. And the hands are fastened to one secure pivot: the great, unchanging heart of our God of love.

Now that's something there's always more than enough of.

The secret of happiness
is to count your blessings
while others are
adding up their troubles.

"Did You Eat Your Lunch?"

~ Sheila Walsh

It was the same deal every day. He prepared himself for it on the walk home from school. Ben and his friend Luke would kick the dusty road with their sandals until clouds formed over their heads, and they would cough and laugh and laugh and cough. Then Ben would rehearse, "Yes, Mom, I ate my lunch. No, Mom, I'm not kidding. Yes, Mom, every bite . . . and it was deeelicious!" When he got home, he knew his mom would laugh at that and make a poor attempt at swatting him with a towel.

It was a mystery to Ben and Luke why mothers felt obliged to be so obsessed with food.

"What I can't understand," Luke said, "is why my mom is always trying to stuff anything that's not moving into me when she hardly eats enough herself to keep a frog alive. I guess it's because Dad says her figure gets more like a pomegranate every day!"

They laughed at that thought as they parted for the day, Ben to one side of the hill, Luke to the other.

"See you tomorrow, Ben. Remember, my mom invited you over to play after school."

"I remember. Bye!"

When he got home, Ben knocked his shoes on the side of the house to shake off most of the sandy dust. "Mom, I'm home!" he called as he went inside. "And I ate my lunch, in case you were wondering!"

Ben was a picky eater and small for his age, so Mary, like all good mothers, worried. "Well, I'm glad to hear it," she said with a smile as she swatted him with a towel.

The next morning as the sun streamed through the open kitchen window, Mary called, "Ben! Are you up yet?"

"Yeah, I'm up," he called back.

"Are you actually out of bed with both feet on the floor?" she asked.

How do mothers know that stuff? Ben wondered as he forced his right foot to join his left foot on the floor.

"I've packed you something special for lunch today," his mom said as Ben dragged his sleepy form into the kitchen. "It's one of your favorites: a couple of pickled fish and a few fresh-baked rolls, hot out of the oven."

"What's 'a few,' Mom?" Ben asked. "Enough to feed the whole school?"

"That's enough of that, young man, and I'll be checking your lunch box when you get home!"

"I'll be a little later today, Mom, remember? Luke's mom invited me over to play for a while."

"That's fine. Just remember your manners and be home before dinner."

As the afternoon shadows began to grow long over Luke's house later that day, Luke's mom said, "It's getting late, Ben. I think you should head home now. Don't forget your lunch box."

Lunch box! Ben thought. *Oh no, I forgot to eat my lunch! Well, maybe I'll meet a hungry dog on the way home.*

Ben wandered down the lane and headed toward the hill that stood between his house and Luke's. It was usually deserted at this time of afternoon, but there was a huge crowd ahead of him. Ben had never seen so many people. *I wonder what's going on?* he thought. He tried to see, but the crowd was too thick. He got down on his hands and knees and made his way through a maze of legs and robes and sandals until he got to the front where a man was talking.

Ben didn't recognize him, but his voice was like a waterfall, soothing and fresh. After a few moments the man stopped. Some of his friends were whispering in his ear. Ben watched their worried expressions. They seemed very cross.

I wonder if I'm going to get in trouble for pushing to the front? he thought, as one of the men came toward the crowd. Then Ben heard him ask if anyone had any food.

Oh great, this is better than giving it to a dog, Ben thought as he stood up to offer his slightly battered lunch. The man didn't seem entirely thrilled with the meager offering, but he took it anyway and gave it to the One who didn't seem worried at all. Ben watched this man named Jesus lift the little lunch up to the sky.

What's he doing with it? Ben wondered, wide-eyed. The crowd became very quiet.

> Taking the five loaves and the two fish and looking up to heaven, he gave thanks and broke the loaves. Then he gave them to his disciples to set before the people. He also divided the two fish among them all.
> —Mark 6:41

Ben could not believe his eyes! He knew what he had in his lunch box. He had five of his mom's little rolls and two pickled fish, *little* pickled fish. But as he watched, this Jesus kept dividing it and dividing it and there was more and more and more. Jesus' friends began distributing the food to the crowd. Ben looked at the man beside him. That one man seemed to have in his hands more bread and fish than Ben had in his lunch box to begin with! Everyone was eating his fill.

> The number of the men who had eaten was five thousand.
> —Mark 6:44

Ben had some of the food too, and it tasted better than anything he could remember from his mom's kitchen. When it was all over and the people began to disperse, Ben watched as some of the men who were with Jesus gathered up baskets full of what was left over. There was enough to feed Ben's whole school for a week!

Wait till I tell Luke about this! he thought. *He'll never believe it.*

Ben hurried home, realizing that he was much later than he had told his mother he would be. He ran into the house.

"Mom! Mom! Where are you?"

"Where am *I?*" his mom said as she came out of the bedroom. "Where have *you* been, young man? Do you know what time it is? I was just about to walk over to Luke's house and fetch you back myself."

"But Mom, I've got something to tell you!"

"It's a little late for that, kiddo. Go on upstairs and wash your face and hands. You look filthy. And what's that on the back of your robe? Have you been rolling on the grass again? How many times do I have to tell you about that!"

"But Mom . . . "

"But nothing. Go on, now. And one more thing . . . did you eat your lunch?"

Whatever you have today
is enough. It might not look
like it to you, but put into
Jesus' hands, it is more
than enough. It is lavish.

Death Threat in Aisle 17

~ Marilyn Meberg

Yesterday I was putting what I thought were the finishing touches on my grandchildren's Easter baskets. Standing back for a moment and eyeballing my handiwork, I realized that something was aesthetically "off." I couldn't quite figure out what it was. Then it dawned on me: the baskets needed that green grasslike stuff to cradle the little chocolate eggs and marshmallow bunnies. I well remembered the annoyance of that green stuff getting stuck in the carpet and nestling between the couch cushions to be discovered months later. As a young mother I lacked the patience for the untimely surfacing of Easter grass; now, as a grandmother, I eagerly went out to buy some.

My, how times have changed! There was no Easter grass as I remembered it. Instead, what was on the shelves was something called "Bunny Batts Funfil." It claims to be a "non-toxic, colorfast, no-mess, and no-loose-strands, flame-retardant" wonder for everything from Easter baskets to tree and plant bedding. Pleased with its color variety and soft feel, I bought a couple of bags. After all, I reasoned, I may decide to spruce up the look of my patio plants with a touch of lavender, pink, yellow, and emerald.

Having accomplished my task, I headed for the checkout counter, meandering through the aisles filled with everything from toilet plungers, car wax, slug bait, and orange juice to a variety of tweezers guaranteed to rid the body of visible nose hair, ear hair, and "unsightly knuckle hair." Mercy! Exiting the aisle devoted to eliminating the embarrassment of incontinence, I shifted my attention to a darling little toddler who was sitting in the front of his mom's shopping cart. His chubby little fists were full of multicolored M&Ms, which he was stuffing into his mouth with obvious pleasure.

The minute he saw me, however, his expression changed. He was apparently offended by the fact that I had grinned at him and winked. With a look of unmistakable hostility, he took a minute to size me up, and then awkwardly flung his fistful of M&Ms in my direction.

Pretending to be afraid, I ducked behind the Attends display, waited a second, and then peeked out at him. His expression had not changed or his aim improved. Once again he attempted to pelt me with M&Ms. Realizing that my playful spirit did nothing but add to his antagonism, I decided to escape down a side aisle before the whole bag of candy was hurled at me.

Amazingly enough, this little fellow's mother was totally unaware of the drama unfolding only a few feet from her. She appeared to be so fully engrossed in the claims of a miracle-working tooth whitener that she completely missed the skirmishes of her tiny warrior.

I have smiled repeatedly over this incident since its occurrence nearly twenty-four hours ago. The experience intrigues me not just because of the ferocity of the baby battler, whom I actually found appealing, but also because it nudges me into some deeper contemplations. For example, other than the possibility that my grin and wink is sufficiently unattractive as to produce acts of violence, I was innocent. I did not deserve the treatment I was getting. Why should my warm-hearted intentions be so furiously rebuffed?

The reason those questions stay with me is that they are not unfamiliar. There have been times when people (other than toddlers) have seemingly misunderstood my motives and reacted negatively. I have left the experience thinking, *What was that all about? I didn't deserve that.* In almost all cases the problem was one of miscommunication and was ultimately solved with a clarifying conversation.

But I have to admit that a few of my experiences with God have fallen into the category of, *What did I do to deserve this? What are you doing? Do you care?* Or worse, *Do you even know what's going on down here?!* Perhaps you've asked the same questions from time to time. When our lives are unexpectedly interrupted with tension, pain, or loss, our tendency is to cast about trying to figure it all out—and thereby hopefully change the outcome of events. At least that's my tendency.

I was in one of those major questioning modes a few months ago as I struggled to grasp the enormity of the health issues that threatened to keep me from fulfilling my speaking and writing obligations for months into the future. If I had been totally honest with God, I'd have confessed to him my fear that my needs might have gotten lost somewhere in the global hubbub. I felt neglected. I was startled, then, to read in my Bible one particularly vulnerable morning:

> "Why do you say, O Jacob, and complain, O Israel, 'My way is hidden from the LORD; my cause is disregarded by my God'?"
> —*Isaiah 40:27*

Frankly, I felt almost embarrassed. My whiny fear that God may have overlooked my needs was addressed in bold print right there in his Word. Not only did he acknowledge my struggle, but he also went on in the next verse to remind me that "his understanding no one can fathom." I'll never be able to figure out God's ways, and certainly it is not within my power to change the events of my life, or their outcome, if God himself has set those events in motion.

But he didn't leave me with my feelings of shame and foolishness. God's not like that. Rather, he pronounced a lavish promise that soothed my soul to the core:

> "He gives strength to the weary
> and increases the power of the weak.
> Even youths grow tired and weary,
> and young men stumble and fall;
> but those who hope in the LORD
> will renew their strength.

They will soar on wings like eagles;
they will run and not grow weary,
they will walk and not be faint."

—*Isaiah 40:29–31*

I took that promise very personally: "He gives strength to weary Marilyn and increases her power when she is weak. She *will* mount up with wings like an eagle." Little did I know as my spirit was encouraged that morning that God would soon literally supply physical strength and unexpected power for my body. Praise his name!

I know my battles aren't over. I know yours aren't either. But isn't it a comfort to know that our God's love is never miserly, never punishing of our secret, doubt-plagued thoughts? He will never pelt us in anger. He will never leave us, even when we whine and throw tantrums in our frustration over what we don't like or don't understand. After all, he knows we're just candy-tossing toddlers at heart.

As a father has compassion
on his children, so the LORD
has compassion on those who
fear him; for he knows how
we are formed, he remembers
that we are dust.

—PSALM 103:13–14

No Flies in Africa

~ Thelma Wells

Have you ever said something that you weren't proud of and found yourself eating your words? On March 12, 2000, I had to eat my words. At least forty people in the Truth Seekers Sunday school class at St. John Missionary Baptist Church had heard me say more than once, "I just can't totally commit myself to the Lord, because he might send me to Africa, and I don't like flies!"

Can you believe that? I had been the teacher of this class for more than a decade. I studied God's Word every week and lived a Christian life, yet I was not totally committed to turning my life over to God's will. Why? Because he might send me to a mission field, and I don't like flies.

Wanna know a secret? Each time I'd make that statement, the Holy Spirit would convict me and I'd feel guilty. But I'd say it again. I said it for years. It was only after a year of struggle that I finally completely and totally gave my life over to the Lord and said, "Whatever, Lord. Send me."

And the Lord sent me to Ghana, West Africa.

What an experience! I didn't have a clue that people lived in such deplorable poverty. I've traveled to many parts of the world and have seen extreme poverty, but nothing like this. Even the largest cities are impoverished. The "haves" have a lot; the "have nots" have little or nothing. Sanitary conditions are virtually nonexistent, and clean water is a luxury. Experiencing this has given me a greater sense of appreciation of the things most of us take for granted, such as:

hot and cold running water
flushing toilets
nutritious meals
sanitized beds and bed linens

ice
comfortable housing
radios, television, telephones, cell phones, computers
air conditioning
washers, dryers, dry cleaning
health and medical resources
paved streets and signal lights
job and career opportunities
modern educational facilities

I could go on, but you get the picture.

I'm really glad God sent me to Africa. Not only did it open my eyes to the conditions of that land, but it also proved again God's lavish love for me. I learned that he never sends us anywhere before he has gone before and cleared the way. I went to Africa, and I don't remember being bothered once by flies. I returned home saying, "There are no flies in Africa."

Do you see why I had to eat my words? I'm certain there are flies in Africa, but they didn't bother me. When I stop to think about that, my heart leaps for joy at how God's love shows up in spite of myself. Even when I should have been committing myself to him without reservation, he put up with me and allowed me to stay healthy and strong so I could get to the place I dreaded and realize his over-the-top grace. Now I can sing this old hymn with a clean, clear, committed heart:

> All to Jesus I surrender,
> All to him I freely give;
> I will ever love and trust him,
> In his presence daily live.
> All to Jesus I surrender,
> Make me, Savior, wholly thine;
> May thy Holy Spirit fill me,
> May I know thy pow'r divine.

All to Jesus I surrender,
Lord, I give myself to thee;
Fill me with thy love and power,
Let thy blessing fall on me.
I surrender all, I surrender all.
All to thee, my blessed Savior,
I surrender all.

Once I surrendered all to Jesus, I found his love to be lavish. He does not stop loving us when we don't surrender to him; we just miss out on some of the blessings he longs to give us. But when we do surrender, he pours out his blessings; he helps us through tough situations; he covers our mistakes and forgives our every sin. He is patient and kind with us. Even when he disciplines us, the punishment is not what we actually deserve. His love is so lavish and free that even when we blow him off, he is steadfast. Look what he did for me! He accepted my repentance, charted my path to the place I said I didn't want to go, and kept me safe, healthy, happy, and productive while there.

Take it from me: Don't waste time holding yourself back from completely surrendering to God. God is love. He made you. He'll keep you. He won't give up on you. He has plans for you that will not harm you, but will give you a bright and glorious future.

The next time you sing, "I Surrender All," let it be the truth. He's waiting for you to surrender all to him so he can shower you with abundance!

"Our courteous Lord does not wish his creatures to lose hope even if they fall frequently and grievously; for our failure does not prevent him loving us."

—JULIAN OF NORWICH

$xoxo\,DP$

~ Luci Swindoll

I hate forwarded e-mail. It's absolutely maddening to me, and while I'd like to be passive about it, I'm not. If you're inclined to send me a cute joke or heart-wrenching story, a perky prayer or silly song, an irresistible piece of wit or wisdom, please ... don't do it. It drives me crazy.

One day I came home from a long trip and there in my in-box were forty-six forwarded messages ... from the same person. *Please.* Even if you want to tell me I'm among the five recipients who just won a box of Snickers waiting to be picked up next door, don't. Even if you're informing me that an airplane has been reserved to fly me to my favorite place in the world if I will just read this message, don't. Even if you have suggestions for the greatest manuscript under my name that will bring me a fortune if I will only click onto something.com, don't. Don't ever, ever forward me anything.

However, let me tell you what I do like in e-mail. I like to get messages that are sweet, kind, encouraging, informative ... and not everlastingly long. I like words from the heart. I like original thoughts. I like information and Scriptures from an understanding, sympathetic friend that will help me on my way in life. And I like clever notes from people who have a way with words. Words that snap and tickle and assure and thrill me to the bone. I like e-mail from Sheila and Annie and Mary and Steve and Traci. They stir my mental "pot" and make me think. They stimulate my imagination and make me laugh. And most of all, they love me. Therefore, they don't ever, ever forward anything to me. That is almost my favorite thing about their cyber correspondence—*no forwarded mail*.

But my classic correspondent, who really has no peers, is Debra Petersen. She fills all the bills. Not only does she e-mail me warm, wonderful personal notes every day from her home in Miami (never anything forwarded), but she also sends me all kinds of snail mail. Hardly a day goes by that I don't find in my mailbox a note or little package from her, housed in a colorful envelope, with my name in big, scrawly, neon writing in her own hand. And I haven't even gotten to the most fun part. Inside that envelope there is apt to be just about anything that speaks of love . . . a cassette tape to encourage me, a card especially chosen just to lift my spirits, a torn-out magazine page with a Post-It note, "I love this" or "Reminds me of you" or "I can just see you in this so I ordered it for you."

Debbie does this kind of thing for countless people, not just me. She keeps the U.S. Postal Service in business. And UPS and FedEx too. Literally. In fact, she told me she has to *stop herself* from sending things to people she loves and those she wants to help. "I love mailing little notes and packages," she says, "because it's like having a visit with people I don't see very often." Can you beat that? She has a room called "the factory" in her small apartment where her multitude of correspondence is handled. (Maybe she has that line from *The Mask* nailed up in there too—"Somebody stop me!")

Let me just wax a minute more about my friend Debbie. She works for Campus Crusade for Christ, but if you've ever been to a Women of Faith conference or one of the "Intensive" meetings on the Friday afternoon before each conference, you've seen her because she's the emcee for those events. It's not as though the girl has nothing to do but haunt the post office. She is wildly busy with a full life of ministry and outreach. It never stops. There are parties and parades and programs for everybody she knows. With personal invitations.

Debra Petersen takes her time with each person she touches. There's the initial encounter of a smile, warm words, and an understanding heart. Then there's the follow-up of a note or Scripture. Ultimately, you receive photos she's taken when she was with you, little presents, maybe candy or books or fresh-baked bread. As she says, "I send anything I think will encourage the person who gets it." Wow! What a giver of love in tiny, daily snippets. Because most people don't get much cheerful e-mail or snail mail, Debbie makes up for the whole world. From her heart. A heart that is sold out to being a light in a dark place. Debbie lavishes love in minutes and seconds and nanoseconds. xoxoDP. How often have I seen that trademark signature at the bottom of one of her notes?

Wanna know how to get on Debbie's correspondence list? I think the truth is you just have to meet her. That seems to be enough. I have no idea how nor why God blessed me with the extravagant attention of this unique friend. I'm truly rich from her simple giving. What Deb does without even knowing it is make me want to be more of a lavish giver myself, in small but consistent ways. She emulates the beauty and reward of doing to others what you want done to you.

The English poet Shelley said, "Familiar acts are beautiful through love," and Debbie lives the truth of that message. She has it engraved across the doorposts of her life, and it is the genuine experience for everybody who enters. Debbie simply loves lavishly and has made the familiar act of correspondence a fine art to lift the hearts of literally hundreds of people. I'm just one of the lucky ones.

I'm going to alter my initial request just this once and close with a personal suggestion to you: you may forward this devotional to anybody you want. xoxoLS.

Thoreau once wrote in his journal, "There is no remedy for love but to love more." Send that in your next e-mail.

Riding on the Rims

~ Marilyn Meberg

he papers described her as the woman who shouted "Praise God, yeah!" as she streaked past the finish line. She was also named the most endearing image from the 104th Boston marathon as she bellowed the National Anthem with a victory wreath on her head, a grin on her face, and radiant delight in her heart. This winner dynamo is Jean Driscoll, the first person ever to win the Boston marathon eight times.

Behind that impressive fact, however, is an inspiring and compelling story. Jean was born with spina bifida. As a child she walked with the aid of crutches, but at age fifteen she was forced to start using a wheelchair. What she had feared would be limiting instead opened up a new world to her. She found that in a wheelchair she could finally play sports: soccer, football, water skiing, basketball, and then racing. In her chair, she can cover 26.2 miles in one hour and thirty-four minutes. In case you need a comparison to grasp that statistic, she is thirty-two minutes faster than the men's able-bodied marathon world record.

I met Jean for the first time several years ago when she wheeled up to my book table in Cincinnati at the conclusion of a Women of Faith conference. I had told the story there of our baby, Joanie, who had been born with spina bifida and died when she was fifteen days old. Jean was touched by my experience and felt God nudged her to introduce herself to me. At the time I had no idea she was a record-breaking world-renowned athlete; I knew simply that she was in a wheelchair and that, as she told me, she too had been born with spina bifida. I found myself deeply touched by this obviously well-educated, bright, vivacious young woman who just happened to be the same age as Joanie would have been.

In addition to the almost instant attachment I felt toward Jean, I also felt a definite "Godness" in our meeting. He had something in mind far greater than just that sweet encounter. We have stayed in touch through periodic phone calls and letters. She never fails to inspire me or move my spirit at a deep level.

God has used her in an especially significant way in the past few months in regard to my own physical restrictions. Jean shared with me her race defeat in 1997 when her chair caught on the MBTA trolley tracks, throwing her timing off completely. Then she lost another competition in a race so close the winner had to be determined by replaying video tape. Utterly discouraged, she went six weeks without training, even contemplating retirement from the sport. I too had wondered if I had "lost the race." Should I just retire, thus freeing Women of Faith to find a replacement speaker?

On the morning of March 7, 2000, the phone rang. It was a jubilant Jean Driscoll calling from Los Angeles to tell me she had just won the L.A. marathon! She was hesitant to call because she knew I was struggling for enough stamina just to walk to my mailbox, and she didn't want to "bother me." I had known she was training for L.A., that she still wasn't sure what God wanted to do with her racing career, and that if she won, it was definitely God's deal. I was thrilled to hear from her and asked for details about the latest victory.

She told me that toward the end of the race, with her opponents well behind her, the carbon fiber wheels on her racing chair gave out; she was reduced to riding on the rims. Determined not to quit or be defeated, she rounded a corner where an unexpected pit crew tore over to her chair, replaced the tires in seconds, and sent her on her way . . . a way that produced a first-place victory.

While I listened to her account I had the strongest sense that God was saying to me: "Listen carefully to this, Marilyn. You, at this moment, are riding on the rims . . . trust me for ultimate victory . . . the race is not over."

I must admit that when I hung up the phone I accused myself of being in la-la land, that my personal identification with Jean's victory probably had more to do with motherly instincts toward her than God's word to me. Nevertheless I couldn't seem to quiet the message that urged me on in a race that God said was not over.

Ten days later, trusting his prompting, I flew to San Jose, California, where I spoke at my first conference of the year. (Three others had already taken place without me.) While God certainly cannot be reduced to a "pit crew," I was deeply aware of him rushing to my aid and then sending me on my way that weekend. In fact, he continues to do just that for me. He makes it possible to do what I do and then cheers me on.

And yet I have to admit that I am constantly challenged by his promise that he "is able to do immeasurably more than all we ask or imagine, according to his power that is at work within us" (Ephesians 3:20). Why in the world I limit the power or provision of the God of the universe is beyond me. I'm embarrassed by my lack of faith in his loving abundance. He states over and over in his Word that "there is no God like me," and I believe that to be true. My problem is receiving and incorporating into my straggling life all that he is and all that he promises to be in my needy state.

This morning I was inspired and even amused as I read a classic piece written by Hannah Whitall Smith. She referenced the passage from 2 Kings 6:17 where God gave Elisha "chariots of fire" to be used in battle, assuring him of victory. According to that passage, not everyone could see the chariots—only those whose eyes God opened. Smith writes:

> Lord, open our eyes so we may see God's chariots of fire. God's chariots are waiting to transport us to places of victory. Once our eyes are opened by God, we will see all the events of our lives, whether great or small, joyful or sad, as a chariot for our souls. Everything that comes to us becomes a chariot the moment we treat it as such.

After reading this I thought, *Well, Marilyn, honey . . . why should you be riding on the rims when you could be streaking about in a chariot of fire?* I've always loved a flashy, fast mode of transportation, and as long as God keeps my eyes open to his lavishly loving provision, I've got one!

Wanna race?

> "I do not at all understand
> the mystery of grace —
> only that it meets us where
> we are but does not leave us
> where it found us."
>
> —ANNE LAMOTT

Watch-Night Service

~ Thelma Wells

M ama, we've decided that we don't want to go to a party or a church service on New Year's Eve. We don't want to be with strangers. We want to be at home with you and Daddy."

Huh? Is this my son on the telephone?

"We'll come over around 10:00 P.M. and play games, talk, and fellowship with each other. At 11:00, I was thinking we could start our own worship service. Little George can pray, I'll read the Scripture, Lesa and Vikki can sing, and Daddy can do whatever he wants. Then, Mama, you can bring us the message. But please limit your talk to ten minutes, okay? You know how you are when you get wound up. Just ten minutes, Mama. How does all that sound to you?"

Ummmm . . . . I actually had my own ideas for New Year's Eve that did not include being at home. Our church was planning a big to-do with a watch-night service and breakfast after midnight. And that's where George and I had thought we'd be. But as I quickly mulled over my son's suggestions, I started to get excited. Just think, our grown children wanted to close out the old year and start the new millennium at home with their *parents.* (Hmmm . . . they were either really afraid of Y2K, or they really love their parents.) I knew they'd been invited to parties and other events, but they wanted to be with us. As a family. I really started liking the idea.

What's a New Year's Eve party without balloons, noisemakers, confetti, fresh flowers, and delicious food? So off I went to get everything ready for this historic night. Then I thought, *At church we would be having testimony service and communion.* So I called each of my children and told them to think about the times in their lives that were the most important turning points for them. I asked my husband to do the same.

Finally, the big day came. December 31, 1999. Beautiful gold and white balloons adorned a magnificent fresh flower centerpiece on the dining table. The tablecloth was accented with gold lamé ribbons, as were the backs of the dining chairs. Gold silverware, gold-ringed goblets, and gold and white dinner and beverage napkins surrounded the gold-trimmed china. White candles set in gold candlesticks illuminated the room. Oh yes, honey, I also wore gold and white. I had found a gold lamé sweater and a long white silk skirt in my closet. Everything was perfectly coordinated and in place.

In my office area where we would play games and have our service, I prepared another table. You guessed it—with white and gold accents. If the aroma of the food cooking on the stove didn't bait everyone, then the scent of the cinnamon spice candles throughout the house would. Music played softly in the background, offering a soothing, sweet atmosphere to the already enchanting evening.

My son's family came early—at 8:30 P.M. They knew I had cooked turnip greens, sweet potatoes, macaroni and cheese, baked chicken, roast pork loin, chitterlings, black-eyed peas, corn bread, peach cobbler, and salad. Yum, yum. Nothing was too good for my family that night—absolutely nothing. I wanted to lavish my love on them so that they would always remember the turn of the century that they'd chosen to spend with each other.

We looked at old pictures and reminisced about the past, played games, and ate. Honey, did we eat! Our worship service started around 11:00. It was so touching to hear each family member give testimony to God's blessings in their lives. Afterward, we shared communion. My son George had just finished praying when the clock struck midnight. Everything was perfect!

As we retired to the den to watch the fireworks on television, I noticed that my son was not in a hurry to leave. He and his wife had said earlier that they would leave right after midnight in order to visit with a few friends. But everybody sat around in the den and got so involved in watching the new millennium festivities that we all lost track of time. We oohed and ahhed at the fireworks, laughed, joked, told stories, and when I finally looked at my watch, it was nearly 5:00 A.M. My whole family was still there! All the excessiveness and extravagance that I had put into making that evening special was worth it!

Isn't that what God does for us? He makes all things beautiful for us. He prepares a table before us, even in the presence of our enemies. He provides the Bread of Life to fill our hungry souls. He illuminates the dark places, and he offers us rest. He promises to withhold no good thing from us, and he gives us people to love. He loves us extravagantly, far beyond anything we can comprehend.

In my humanity, I was limited in what I could do to create the perfect festive experience for my children and grandchildren. Perhaps if I had to plan the evening over, I would do something different. But God never has to redo or undo anything for us. Every event and experience is perfectly created for our edification. God gives us the freedom each day to come into his presence and enjoy sweet fellowship with him. Often, when we don't come voluntarily, he pays us a visit, because he never wants us to think we're far from his thoughts.

> How precious to me are your thoughts, O God!
> How vast is the sum of them!
> Were I to count them, they would outnumber the
>   grains of sand.
> When I awake, I am still with you.
>
> —*Psalm 139:17*

Next time you have a moment's doubt about how much God loves you, meditate on those verses. Bask in his infinite attention and steadfast presence. Glory in his lavish love. And then give it away.

Honey, you are
LOVED . . . so far
beyond your imagining!

"Show Me the Love!"

~ Barbara Johnson

I f you ever saw the movie *Jerry McGuire*, you'll recall the Oscar-winning performance of Cuba Gooding, Jr., who played the high-flying, cocky football player Rod Tidwell. McGuire, a sports agent whose only client is Tidwell, is trying hard to land a deal for the athlete (who should be happy that *anyone* is willing to represent him).

In a memorable scene Tidwell makes it clear that the only thing that will convince him he's valued is cold, hard cash. "Show me the money!" he shouts—a challenge that became a popular mantra throughout America for months after the movie premiered in 1996.

I frequently hear from people who are baffled by a loved one's disinterest in the gospel or outright hostility toward Christians. "How can I witness to so-and-so?" they ask. "How can I convince people that they should give God a chance?"

And I wonder . . . are the people these folks are trying to "witness" to and persuade simply waiting to see evidence of the kind of love that is irresistible once it's experienced? Are they shouting inside, "Show me the love!"?

I know a lot of times it's not that simple. But, I believe, often it is. In his great treatise on love, the apostle Paul said, "If I speak in the tongues of men and of angels, but have not love, I am only a resounding gong or a clanging cymbal" (1 Corinthians 13:1). Sometimes I wonder what the people we "love" are actually hearing when we're trying so hard to speak for God. Are they really getting the message that God's love is boundless, all-inclusive, personal, and lavish beyond description? Or are they hearing *Clang! Clang! Gong!*

In one of her many writings, Mother Teresa said, "Be kind and merciful. Let no one ever come to you without leaving better and happier. Be the living expression of God's kindness: kindness in your face, kindness in your smile, kindness in your warm greeting . . . To children, to the poor, to all who suffer and are lonely, give always a happy smile. Give them not only your care, but also your heart."

Sometimes it's easier to give someone "the answer" than it is to really give our hearts, isn't it? After all, they might reject our hearts. Better to just try harder to get our point across. After all, didn't Jesus say to go and "make" disciples (Matthew 28:19)?

Yes, but how did he intend for us to go about that great commission? "A new command I give you," Jesus said. "Love one another. As I have loved you, so you must love one another. By this all men will know that you are my disciples, if you love one another" (John 13:34–35). In other words, *show*, don't just *tell*.

I love how British novelist Anita Brookner describes "real love" as a pilgrimage. "It happens when there is no strategy, but it is very rare because most people are strategists."

Do we really need to try so hard to "get" people to "get it" (the gospel)? Or do we just need to show them the love? As Ruth Bell Graham so wisely reflects, "It's my job to love Billy. It's God's job to make him good."

In order to *show* love rather than just tell about it, Paul says that our love must be sincere. "Be devoted to one another in brotherly love," he says. "Honor one another above yourselves" (Romans 12:9–10). Think about how you can do that today in the lives of the people God brings across your path. Keep it simple. It doesn't take a rocket scientist to figure out how to shower someone with the lavish love of God . . .

- Call someone who has enriched your life and say, "I'm so grateful for your friendship. Thank you for being you."
- Take to lunch someone you've been trying to "witness" to, and just spend the time encouraging her in the midst of whatever life is dishing out to her these days. Say, "I care. I'm here for you."
- Drop a pretty greeting card in the mail to someone you've been resentful toward and say, "I'm thinking of you and

wishing you the very best today." (You'll be amazed at how your attitude will shift!)

- Tell someone who's done something nice for you how deeply you appreciate his kindness. *Show* him how grateful you are by doing something nice for *him*—not as "payment," but as an expression of the always abundant, lavish love of God. You can "afford" to share it!
- Simply walk in Christ's footsteps.

Be imitators of God, therefore, as dearly loved children and live a life of love, just as Christ loved us and gave himself up for us as a fragrant offering and sacrifice to God.

—Ephesians 5:1–2

Every time you interact with another human being, remember that their heart's deepest cry, like yours, is "Show me the love!" The apostle John makes it crystal clear: "This is how we know what love is: Jesus Christ laid down his life for us. And we ought to lay down our lives for our brothers" (1 John 3:16).

God showed you the love, lavishly. Now you show others, so they'll know whose you are.

> "How great is the love the Father has lavished on us, that we should be called children of God! And that is what we are!"
>
> —1 JOHN 3:1

Outlandish
Love

Dear Friends,

If you have known the six of us for a while, or are just getting started, you won't be surprised to know that we all love the outlandish. Marilyn and Luci have an off-the-wall sense of humor. I follow them around like a lost dog because they make me laugh. My son Christian's heart is painted with wonderful pictures that Patsy and Barbara have placed there through loving gifts and stories. Thelma has lived through outrageous circumstances but has come out smelling like a rose.

All of us have had the opportunity to live through some difficult and, at times, heartbreaking circumstances. The situations have been different, but the outcome in our hearts is the same. We are absolutely convinced that God's love is outlandish — not only odd (beyond human reason), fantastic (beyond believing), and even bizarre (constantly surprising and shocking), but also extraordinary, eccentric, exceptional, unusual, outrageous!

The sovereign, holy God of the universe invites you and me to come to him exactly as we are. (If that's not outlandish, I don't know what is.) Perhaps as you look at your life at the moment, you don't feel loved or lovable. But feelings are unreliable; God's Word is immovable. And his Word promises that you are loved, accepted, treasured.

So come with us now as we take a closer look at the outlandish love of God. Knowing my friends as I do . . . hold on to your hats!

Love,

Sheila

Nothin' Says Lovin' Like Somethin' from the Oven

~ Luci Swindoll

I love to cook. Well, maybe not *love,* but strongly like. There's something about creating wonderful dishes in the kitchen that makes me feel alive. I'm enhancing my health. I'm saving money. I'm aiding the war effort. You get the picture. In the words of Martha Stewart, cooking is *a good thing.*

I don't pretend to be as skilled as my two gourmet friends Ruth or Kurt, but I make a mean soufflé. Don't ever ask me to make bread, though. I did that once for the first and last time. It was such a failure I'm now writing a book entitled *One Loaf, That's All I Knead.* My worst moment in the kitchen.

Oh, and then there's that time Daddy and I made a pecan pie. Long after Mother died (who was fabulous with pies . . . and bread, I might add), I said to my dad, "Let's make a pecan pie. It's a beautiful fall day and we'll pool our resources and whip out the world's prettiest pie . . . it'll be fun." He loved the idea, shelled the pecans . . . and I made the crust.

Oh. My. Gosh. Have you ever *made crust?* Let me give you a word of advice: don't. It's an impossible task. I thought defrosting a refrigerator was tough, or cleaning the oven, but making, baking, scraping crust is much, much worse. I must have either left something out or put something in that caused me to wind up with a small plate of cement. When that pie (which actually looked pretty good upon completion) came out of the oven and we tried to cut it, both Daddy and I used a chisel, literally, to remove it from the pan. Not even one pecan budged. Nada.

But . . . you know what I totally enjoyed about that pie? The fun we had making it! The whole idea of *me and Daddy* trying to follow in Mother's footsteps was outlandish in the first place. We laughed our heads off, sang, horsed around. Who cares if our masterpiece looked like a Frisbee?

The well-known, incomparable chef Wolfgang Puck once said, "Cooking is my *kinderspiel*—my child's play. You can make it yours, too. And while you're cooking, don't forget to share and laugh. Laugh a great deal, and with much love—it enhances the flavor of food."

Ain't it the truth? Lovin' from the oven, right there.

Both Ruth and Kurt have told me that a full meal can be made effectively in twenty minutes, and who am I to doubt them? I've eaten at each of their tables many times and reveled in the delicious food. But the sweetest thing about being their guest is observing the joy with which they cook and entertain. Nothing is too hard and nobody is in the way. Everybody wants to be in the kitchen. That's where all the creativity takes place, the best laughs, the most extraordinary moments. As guests, we may not want to do the cooking, but we want to watch the experts.

In Wolfgang Puck's cookbook *Modern French Cooking*, he talks about the joy he finds in cooking and the men and women who influenced him in his culinary career—his beloved grandmother, famous French chefs, restaurant owners. He tells about the poetic approach they had toward the fine art of preparing a meal, the confidence they poured into him, and the freedom they gave him to grow and make mistakes. He refers to the *love* they had for cooking and for their guests.

I realize most of us who cook are doing so for a family. Everybody's hungry and eager for a good meal; obviously that atmosphere has the potential to create tension. But, trust me on this, when the meal is finished and the table is clear, rare is the person who's going to ponder the recipe used or why the dishes didn't match. More likely they're going to remember conversations, laughter, zany moments, and the way they were treated.

What is the legacy you are leaving through the domain of your kitchen? Will people remember they were encouraged in that room, or criticized? Will they recall the fun or the fights? Will they think of sharing recipes and culinary efforts with good humor or one-upmanship? We, as women, have a splendid opportunity to impart the love of Christ from a simple dining table or kitchen stove. It doesn't take a lot—just remembering our *kinderspiel*—our "child's play."

I asked Marilyn one Christmas to give me her favorite recipe. We had been working together, having a great time as we fixed dinner. Without the slightest hesitation she said, "Okay, write this down"—and I did.

Marilyn's Favorite Recipe for Smooth and Satiny Brown Gravy

4 c. flour	1 c. fruit cocktail (with liquid)
1 T. white pepper	1 tsp. nutmeg
3 T. salt	1 c. arrowroot
2 tsp. cinnamon	1 c. raisins

Take a 5-lb. mallet, place in palm of right hand. Methodically coerce lumps into satiny submission. Allow one hour for smooth and satiny effect. May be made ahead of time and stored until the return of Christ. Serve in silver, which enhances flavor. Serves 23 guests, give or take 12. (Aunt Rebecca wanly commented after four bites: "Something's amiss, but . . ."—after which she slipped quietly into a coma.)

I cannot tell you how I *love, love, love* that outlandish recipe. It's mine forever and I've read it a thousand times. I jotted it in my journal in 1987. When I'm fed up with problems and people and life, I whip it out and read it again. I may even make that gravy someday and not only slip into a coma, but die a happy woman.

Pick up a copy of
Sophia Loren's cookbook,
Recipes & Memories. It's not
only full of great-looking food,
but a bushel of love and
affection as well.

The Hair Prayer

~ Marilyn Meberg

I magine this ... Even as I write these words, there is a flotilla of "Rugrats" doll heads floating toward Alaska. (How about that for a piece of information I can toss out during a conversational lull?) A month ago, tens of thousands of Tommy Pickles doll heads designed for a Mattel's animated TV show managed to fall overboard from the ship that carried them toward their destination. They are now making their current-propelled way to various destinations in the world. Two heads have already been found in Oregon, one in Washington, and thirteen in British Columbia's Queen Charlotte Islands. A scientist who was put on "doll alert" and tracks ocean currents says a big patch of heads is expected to bump onto the shores of Alaska anytime.

Apparently the heads are about the size of a coconut without a husk. Can you imagine anything more unnerving than strolling along a shoreline somewhere, thinking your usual deep, contemplative thoughts, when suddenly a pickle head emerges from the water's edge, rolls awkwardly toward your sandy sneakers, and then stares woodenly up at you? *Am I really seeing this?* you might wonder. *Maybe I really did flunk that Rorschach test.* At that point of self-doubt it would be a comfort if a few thousand more heads surfaced so that at least you could say with confidence, "Yes, I really am seeing this!" Of course, the how and why of the strange experience would present a new array of challenges.

Much as I'd love it, nothing as outlandishly quirky as a marooned pickle head has ever come into my line of vision. But there have been many times when I've second-guessed what I saw and speculated about my ability to accurately "get the picture."

My most recent experience with this was three and a half weeks ago. I was talking to God about something which rather embarrassed me to even bring up but which was a sufficiently strong concern for me to say, "Okay, I'm going to pray about this even though I think the subject indicates I am a shallow woman whose priorities need realignment." Let me give you a little background on what prompted my prayer.

One of my physical responses to the poison still working its way out of my system has been hair loss. All my life I have been basically hair and teeth—no face, just hair and teeth. But I was fast becoming just teeth. Now, in the grand scheme of recovery I felt the hair concern was minor, but when I brought it up to God he didn't indicate that it was minor at all. In fact, I was stunned by the divine response I sensed clearly in my spirit.

The oft-repeated Old Testament phrase stated by God to his people and prophets is, ". . . that you might know that I am God." In other words, God would do something for his people that only God could do: part the Red Sea; defeat the giant, Goliath, through the boy, David; raise up a field of bones to life; produce torrential rains from a previously cloudless sky to overwhelm the worshippers of the idol, Baal, etc. God would conclude these various demonstrations of his miraculous power by explaining, ". . . that you might know that I am God." When I prayed my hair prayer, there was the immediate inner assurance that hair would indeed come, for the purpose of Marilyn "knowing" that God is God.

I must add that there was another little desire I threw out to God during the hair prayer. I asked God if hair growth could occur in time for our yearly Women of Faith photo shoot, scheduled for only three weeks hence. Quite frankly, I thought I was really pushing it, but asked anyway.

Of course, the enemy of our souls loves to "undo" our faith in God's promises to us, so it wasn't long before I was questioning what God actually meant what he assured me: yes, it was okay for me to pray for hair and, yes, he was going to provide it. I began to second-guess not only the divine invitation to bring my every care to him

(Psalm 55:22), but also to doubt the assurance that he was going to give me exactly what I'd asked for. After all, children and adults are dying of cancer, people are confined to wheelchairs, strokes reduce once-vigorous people to needy dependency, refugees displaced and traumatized by ethnic cleansing desperately struggle just to survive . . . and I have the nerve to ask God for mere hair in the midst of such crushing human affliction? In short, I quickly condemned myself as well as my prayer as inexcusably vain and utterly inappropriate.

However, in spite of my embarrassed inner protests, the contrasting message "that you may know that I am God" continued to reverberate in my spirit.

As the days passed I noticed that the sink was increasingly clear of the little hair nests that normally nestled in the drain following every shampoo. One morning I peered into the mirror and tentatively asked out loud, "Am I seeing what I think I'm seeing?" Dozens and dozens of wiry little hair sprouts were poking out all over my pink scalp. Surely not . . . surely yes. Incredible! How can that be . . . why would God . . . you mean he *really* . . . ?

I flew to the photo shoot last week with my wildly sprouting and totally unmanageable new hair. The recent growth was undeniable. So was God's fulfilled promise. And so is my gratitude. My dear friends—Luci, Patsy, Thelma, Barbara, and Sheila—listened eagerly as I told them about the hair prayer and God's response. Not one of them seemed to think I'd careened off my spiritual trolley tracks, but instead entered completely into my blessing. They also voiced a strong "no" to the wig I had purchased when I feared God might need a backup plan for the photo shoot. They all said my own new hair was far better. (I could swear I heard God chuckle over that.)

I cannot even begin to understand or explain the divine "why" of this hair experience. My husband died at age fifty-two of cancer; our baby died when she was two weeks old; scores of people prayed, but God did not choose to do what I longed for. Why not? Does he love me more now than he did then? No. God simply does what he does because he's God. I'll never figure him out. The hair prayer experience just reminded me again: "'My thoughts are completely different from yours,' says the LORD. 'And my ways are far beyond anything you could imagine. For just as the heavens are higher than the earth, so are my ways higher than your ways and my thoughts higher than your thoughts'" (Isaiah 55:8–9 NLT).

Here's the only thing I do know about the hair deal: The hair is merely something visible that God is using to tangibly assure me of his divine power, his sovereign design to raise me up again in spite of how I feel or even look, and the outlandish lengths to which he'll go to reassure me of his love and power. Why he goes to all that trouble is beyond me, but he states clearly: "I am God and there is no other; I am God, and there is none like me. I make known the end from the beginning, from ancient times, what is still to come. I say: My purpose will stand, and I will do all that I please" (Isaiah 46:9–10).

When God says his purpose will stand and that he does what he pleases, my part in it all is to sit back humbly, receive whatever it is he plans for me, and *believe* in what I see. Right now his divine touch is impossible not to see . . . it's sprigging up all over my head! Why? " . . . that you might know, Marilyn . . . that you might know."

> "Even to your old age and gray hairs I am he, I am he who will sustain you. I have made you and I will carry you; I will sustain you and I will rescue you."
>
> —ISAIAH 46:4

Is It Love . . . or Is It the Flu?

~ Sheila Walsh

Barry and I had been dating for over a year, and tonight we were going to one of our favorite Laguna Beach restaurants. Italian. Inside my size six or eight body (depending on the time of the month, new Ben and Jerry's ice cream flavors, the situation in Bosnia, etc.), there is a robust Italian woman longing to get out.

I knew Barry would pick me up around 7:00, so I had just enough time to finish an essay for my C. S. Lewis class at Fuller Seminary. I was in no great rush. We were far beyond the trying-to-look-perfect-on-every-date stage. (That lasted about four dates for me . . . too much work.)

Next time I looked at the clock I saw it was almost seven. I changed out of my jeans and put on a dress. I'm not much of a dress woman. My favorite uniform is blue jeans, a white shirt, and no shoes. If I do wear shoes, then they usually have four-inch heels. I believe it goes back to my primal fear of God calling me to be a missionary in lands with great hairy beasties. In my subconscious mind I determined that if God was scanning the earth looking for good missionary stock he would say, "Well, we can't send her. Look at her shoes!" So although dresses are not my thing (I have fat knees—honestly!), I made some concessions for Barry.

At seven on the dot the doorbell rang. I opened the door, still struggling to get into shoe number two, and took a good look at my boyfriend.

"You don't look well," I said. "Are you feeling all right?"

"Yes! Sure! I'm fine," he replied, pacing the apartment like a woman with a wallet full of cash the day before Nordstrom's big sale.

"We don't have to go out," I said. "I could cook something and we could watch a movie."

"No! I mean . . . I'm fine. Really, I'm fine. Let's go."

It usually took fifteen minutes to drive from my apartment to downtown Laguna, but on a busy Friday night all bets were off. Barry seemed to be getting worse as we waited in traffic. I felt his forehead.

"You're hot," I said. "I think you might have the flu. It's going around, you know."

"Really, I promise I don't have the flu. I might throw up, but don't worry . . . I don't have the flu."

We finally found a parking spot and made our way into the bustling restaurant. Those innocents without reservations had no hope, but Barry had planned ahead. We were shown to our table and I remember thinking as I watched him sweat, *I wonder if he wants to break up with me? If he does, then I'm definitely having the tiramisu. Two of them!*

The waiter gave us our menus. I set mine down on the table for a moment, enjoying the boisterous Italian atmosphere.

"Aren't you going to order?" Barry barked.

"Man, you're cranky tonight," I said. "Here, have some bread. Your blood sugar must be off."

He glared at me. Finally, to avoid an international incident, I picked up my menu to look for the most fattening item. Cranky men do not deserve thin girlfriends.

I couldn't understand the menu at first. There wasn't a cream sauce in sight. Then I realized that it wasn't a menu at all, but a typed-out proposal.

I love you with all my heart. Will you marry me?

I stared at the words for a moment. Then I looked up and found myself staring into a television camera.

"Am I on *Candid Camera?*" I asked.

"Well, answer him!"

The voice came from behind me. It was my best friend, Marlene. I suddenly realized that the restaurant was full of our friends, all waiting for my answer.

I turned back to look at Barry, but he wasn't there. He was on his knees beside me holding out the most beautiful ring imaginable. There was a moment of silence. All eyes were on us.

"Yes," I answered. "Of course I will marry you." Everyone cheered and clapped.

Later that evening as Barry was dropping me off at my apartment I asked him, "What would you have done if I'd said no? I mean, you had a camera crew; all our friends were watching. It could have been mortifying!"

"You are worth the risk," he said simply as he kissed me good night.

I often think about that when I meet women across the country. One thing we all have in common is a deep desire for love that says, "You are worthwhile. You are priceless. You are worth risking for." We have a deep well that we long to have filled with significance and a sense of belonging. We want to be cherished.

I don't know how romantic your life is or how many sweet moments and memories you have tucked into the satin pockets of your heart. But I know this: you are adored and cherished by God. Human romance is wonderful, but it comes and goes. God's passionate love for us never wanes. It's not affected by whether we are size six or twenty-six. And the outlandish lengths to which God will go to prove his love are beyond any scheme a human being—even one as willing to risk as my husband—could dream up.

> This is how God showed his love among us: He sent his one and only Son into the world that we might live through him. This is love: not that we loved God, but that he loved us and sent his Son as an atoning sacrifice for our sins.
>
> —1 John 4:9–10

I'd say that's a pretty outlandish plan. What a risk he took! I mean, we could have all said, "No, thanks." And many have.

I'm so glad I said "YES" to God's invitation to an everlasting love. How about you?

Every time you look in
the mirror, remember that
you are treasured and loved
by the ultimate Lover.

Peculiarities

~ Patsy Clairmont

Jesus' conspicuously unconventional behavior caused others to take a second gander. I mean, this humble man made divine proclamations that caused even the clergy to huddle. Dismayed by Jesus' bizarre ways and his influence on the populace, the religious leaders plotted his demise.

What is it about "different" that threatens us so? We seem to have a need for things to be as we've always known them to feel safe—even if the way they've been ain't all that spiffy. And heaven forbid if anyone thinks *us* odd.

I've noted those hesitant qualities in myself at times. The unknown, the peculiar, and the strange are off-putting.

Folks were abuzz when the off-putting Bethlehem man showed up in their town and healed the afflicted on the Sabbath. Jesus left people aghast and in awe as he created outlandish controversy wherever he went. He deliberately stepped across traditional lines, and he did so in such miraculous and peculiar ways: turning water into wine, touching lepers, forgiving prostitutes, raising the dead, keeping company with social outcasts, and casting out demons—to name just a few of his startling choices. Jesus had a *way*, and it certainly wasn't the people's way or, come to think of it, our way either.

Thank heavens Christ came to rescue us from our smallness, our emptiness, our busyness, our loneliness, and our sinfulness. Left on my own, without the Lord's intervention, I squander precious time, I hold onto grudges as if they were my best friends, I pass judgments as generously as police officers hand out tickets, and I plump up my weaknesses like a down pillow.

I'm grateful Christ hasn't left us to flail about in our inadequacies, but instead he guides us toward transformation. Just listen to some of the unnatural changes that are necessary if we are to be like him.

> "Love your enemies." —Luke 6:27

Hello? I don't do that great of a job loving those I truly care about, so what are the chances I'm going to embrace some bozo who gets on my last nerve? I'll tell you: absolutely zero without Christ.

> "Pray for those who persecute you." —Matthew 5:44

Last week some lady took the parking spot I was waiting for, and I wanted to deck her. (I'm not boasting; I'm confessing.) Imagine if she had committed some *really* annoying act! Why, I'd probably be doing community service for the next few years.

> "Do not store up for yourselves treasures on earth." —Matthew 6:19

Uh-oh. Does that include my teapot collection? Or my grandmother's ring? Surely that doesn't mean my collection of children's books? Or my antique desk?

Those are just a few of the character issues Christ wants to address in us. He longs for us to experience radical transformation of what comes naturally. Isn't that outlandish? All I can say is it's a good thing our God is big because, if we're going to be that different from our human nature, he's going to be very busy. Talk about a full-time job!

Do you think the Lord's ways seem outlandish to us because just capturing a glimpse of him causes us to gasp with wonder? Because he's so much more than we can think or imagine?

Perhaps that's how Isaiah felt when he saw the Lord sitting on a throne, high and lofty. Listen in to Isaiah's response: "Woe to me! . . . I am ruined! For I am a man of unclean lips, and I live among a people of unclean lips, and my eyes have seen the King, the LORD

Almighty" (Isaiah 6:5). Seeing the Lord caused Isaiah to realize his own unfit condition, for it stood in direct contrast to the Lord of hosts' holiness.

Yes, the Lord makes seemingly outrageous requests of us. But when we see him as he is, we long to be different, truly transformed—even outlandish, like him.

> "*Now, therefore, if ye will obey my voice indeed, and keep my covenant, then ye shall be a peculiar treasure unto me.*"
>
> —EXODUS 19:5 KJV

Love Everflowing

~ Barbara Johnson

Every single minute of every single day, half a million tons of water wash over Niagara Falls. The everflowing river is a given. But in the middle of the night on March 29, 1948, the flow suddenly stopped. According to newspaper reports at the time, people living within the sound of the falls were awakened by the overwhelming silence. They believed it was a sign that the world was coming to an end. For thirty long hours they waited and wondered before the flow resumed.

What happened? Apparently strong winds set the ice fields in Lake Erie in motion. Tons of ice jammed the Niagara River near Buffalo and stopped the flow of the river, until the ice shifted again more than a whole day later.

Talk about outlandish! No one would have, could have, ever predicted such a startling event. But life is full of outrageous surprises, isn't it? Some of them are delightful: like the box of ten thousand BBs my resourceful husband brought home for me when I needed only one to drop in my makeup bottle to keep it from getting thick and gooey.

But then there are those bizarre twists on our path that become our worst nightmares. Like the phone call I got in 1968 telling me my son Stephen had been killed in action in Vietnam. And the other phone call I got in 1973, informing me that my son Tim had been killed by a drunk driver. And the many phone calls I never got, for eleven long years, when my gay son and I were estranged and I thought my heart was shattered beyond repair.

What I keep learning along this outlandishly unpredictable journey called life is: (1) we can't predict (or control) the unpredictable, so we might as well stick a geranium in our hats and be happy; (2) we can trust that nothing, absolutely nothing, can stop the flow of God's boundless love into our lives. No fluke in the weather or obstacle in our path can keep God's love from reaching us, even when the world seems to be coming to an end.

Trust me, I've been there. Trust Job, he's been there too. "Why did I not perish at birth, and die as I came from the womb?" (Job 3:11). Talk about a dark hour! Thousands upon thousands of people have "been there"—seemingly at that point of no return . . . frozen . . . out of the flow. But then, sometimes suddenly, most often slowly, they get back on center, "thaw," inch from despair back to faith, and stand strong again under the waterfall of God's everflowing love.

The apostle Paul, who certainly knew what it felt like to be out of the flow and at the end of his rope, summed up the bottom-line truth of our lives so beautifully when he recorded with utter confidence one of the most beautiful passages in all of Scripture.

> Who shall separate us from the love of Christ? Shall trouble or hardship or persecution or famine or nakedness or danger or sword? . . .
>
> No, in all these things we are more than conquerors through him who loved us. For I am convinced that neither death nor life, neither angels nor demons, neither the present nor the future, nor any powers, neither height nor depth, nor anything else in all creation, will be able to separate us from the love of God that is in Christ Jesus our Lord.
>
> —*Romans 8:35, 37–39*

Dear one, I urge you to read this love letter of faith and encouragement—the whole of Romans 8—over and over again . . . and again . . . until you become "convinced," with Paul, that *nothing* can stop the flow of God's tenacious, boundless, outlandish, wildly extravagant love into your life. So much in life is unpredictable, but God's love is certain.

The love of God toward you
is like the Amazon River
flowing down to water
a single daisy.

Tailor-Made Love

~ Marilyn Meberg

During a particularly discouraging day in regard to my recent health challenges, I was attempting to focus on God's power, his faithfulness, and his love for me. I tried memorizing Scripture (Deuteronomy 33:26–27, to be exact), but couldn't seem to latch onto the power or comfort of the words. Neither could I get them to stay in my head. The result was an insidiously growing sense of despair.

Muttering "I need a distraction," I left my reading chair and turned on the TV in the living room. I caught the beginning of a fascinating and comforting discussion on the benefits of positive thinking (all biblical reminders), the capacity of the human body to heal itself, and the need to replenish it with natural herbs and vitamins. (The infomercial person just happened to sell those products, and I could even get them for myself by calling an 800 number flashing on my screen. Now wasn't that convenient?)

My spirit lifted at the reminder that my body has enormous Creator-provided potential to get well when afflicted. Physical regeneration is so often possible because of the way that God formed the human body, cell by cell!

I marveled at the outlandishness of God's love for me as he empathized with my inability to appropriate his Word that afternoon and sent me to my TV instead to watch exactly what I *could* grasp and claim. In so doing he did not chastise me, belittle me, or fill me with guilt. Instead he comforted me ... ministered to me ... assured me that I need not despair.

I am overwhelmed by God's meeting me where I was that afternoon instead of insisting I meet him where he is. The verses I couldn't seem to get a handle on earlier suddenly filled my soul with glorious comfort.

"There is no one like the God of Jerusalem—
He descends from the heavens
In majestic splendor to help you.
The eternal God is your Refuge,
And underneath are the everlasting arms.
He thrusts out your enemies before you.
It is he who cries, 'Destroy them!'"

—*Deuteronomy 33:26–27* TLB

I would understand if you said to me, "Are you kidding, Marilyn—you mean to say that an *infomercial* spoke to you more meaningfully than those huge promises of God?" I'm embarrassed to say that's exactly what happened. But what is notable is not my weakness or even faithlessness at that moment. What is notable— outlandish!—is God's complete lack of ego in meeting my need. What tender grace he extended to me. The God who promises to be my eternal refuge, as well as wipe out my enemies, could certainly have been a bit put off with my "yeah, but . . ." inability to believe in his ability to heal and restore. But that's what so amazes me about God. His love is tailor-made for my need. He never filters his love and help through the human system based upon performance and merit. My human lack did not limit his divine provision. Why? Because of his boundless love!

The whole concept of a personal, tailor-made love expression of God for me has never been more tangible than with the timing of that infomercial. I know that sounds a trifle crazy, but God knows I've always been an advocate of natural herbs and foods as well as vitamin supplements. Knowing that about me, the information in that infomercial was a "fit" for my predisposed inclinations. God also knows my desire to maintain positive mental and emotional atti-tudes, such as those described by the apostle Paul: "Finally, brethren, whatever is true, whatever is honorable, whatever is right, whatever is pure, whatever is lovely, whatever is of good repute, if there is any

excellence and if anything worthy of praise, dwell on these things"
(Philippians 4:8 NASB).

Now, two and a half months after that outlandishly personal love-
touch from God, I have successfully memorized the Deuteronomy
verses as well as begun to truly internalize the magnitude of those
incredible promises.

Incidentally, you may be wondering if I called the 800 number
flashing on the bottom of my TV screen during the infomercial. Of
course I did! Am I swallowing the stuff? Sure. Does it work? I don't
know . . . it sure doesn't hurt. But I'll tell you what I know for sure:
I experienced a dimension of God's tailor-made, nonjudgmental,
outlandish love for me in a way I'll never forget.

Another passage I've memorized is tailor-made for me too. But
I'll be glad to share it with you!

> I love the LORD, for he heard my voice;
> he heard my cry for mercy.
> Because he turned his ear to me,
> I will call on him as long as I live.
> The cords of death entangled me,
> the anguish of the grave came upon me;
> I was overcome by trouble and sorrow.
> Then I called on the name of the LORD:
> "O LORD, save me!"
> The LORD is gracious and righteous;
> our God is full of compassion.
> The LORD protects the simplehearted;
> when I was in great need, he saved me.
> Be at rest once more, O my soul,
> for the LORD has been good to you.
>
> —*Psalm 116:1–7*

Instead of being surprised when God appears in outlandish ways . . . expect him! He wants to send you a love note — tailor-made, just for you.

What's in a Name?

~ Thelma Wells

Have you ever been driving along and saw something that caused you to do a double-take? *Whah . . . ? What was that?* That's the way it was for me when I visited Ghana.

It started when I noticed a sign on a taxi in front of us: "Jesus Cares Taxi." *Okay,* I thought. *You're right. He does care. That's nice that the cab owner recognizes that.* But as I looked out the window to my right, I saw another sign. Then I noticed other vans and vehicles passing us with all kinds of Christian wording and Scriptures written on them.

That's odd, I thought. *We don't do anything like this in America. Why do they do this?* I realize that our cultures are very, very different. But who ever heard of writing stuff like that all over cars and buildings? *Can't they think of something better to name their businesses?* I wondered. *Are they fanatics, or what? Has someone ordered them to do this?*

I saw so many signs that I started writing them down. My personal mission became to record as many of these signs as possible. But I saw so many words and phrases that expressed people's praise and thanksgiving to God that my hand grew tired of writing before I'd recorded a fraction of what I witnessed.

As we drove through downtown Accra, the capital of Ghana, I saw still more signs. I finally asked our World Vision host, Agnes, why the people did this.

"Christians in Ghana love the Lord and want everyone to know it," she replied. "This is our way of spreading the gospel. We want to carry the message of the saving power of Jesus Christ everywhere we go. We want to praise him in all we do, and we want people to know that we bless the Lord at all times. Some people believe that if they name their businesses after the Lord, they will be successful.

Also, others display these signs as evidence that they denounce other religions, because God is greater."

The ride from Accra to Kumaski to Atebubu to Coast Cape was a challenge. Picture me riding along, bumping and bouncing up and down over the dirt roads and jungle terrain, frantically recording all the signs I saw on shacks, dumpsters, modest businesses, and cars. Would you dare name your business one of these sixty names I saw in Ghana, even though you love the Lord?

1. Nant Nante Yie (Walk Well with the Lord)
2. Nhyira Nka Boafo (Blessed Be My Helper)
3. Blessed Beauty Shop
4. Garden of Eden Sports Shop
5. Mustard Seed Prayer Center
6. Oh! Yes Jesus (bus)
7. Salon De Hope
8. Baby Jesus Nursery School
9. God Is Able Fashion Center
10. End Times Professional Studio
11. Peace Art Store
12. Nso Ya (Nothing is too difficult for God. When you get him, you are satisfied!)
13. Jesus of the Deep Forest Books
14. God's Time = Mere (The Best Time)
15. Pentecost Fire (taxi)
16. Oh Jesus! (taxi)
17. Emmanuel (a common name used on many businesses and vehicles)
18. God Is So Good (retail store)
19. Ays Fa Firi Wo (Father Forgive Them)
20. Divine Love Art Centre
21. The Merciful Lion Photographs (photos on tombstones)
22. Thank U Jesus (retail store)

23. God Is So Wonderful Fashions
24. Prince of Peace Snacks
25. The Name of the Lord Is a Strong Tower
    New Hope Farm
26. El Shaddai (Lord God Almighty) Center
27. Adoni (age to age you're still the same by the power of your name) Complex
28. King Jesus Cares Nursery
29. Peace and Love Shop
30. All Hail the Power of Jesus' Name (business)
31. Blessed Assurance (business)
32. All Creation Praise Jehovah (truck)
33. Jesus Saves Pharmacy
34. In God's Time Electrical Repair
35. Jesus Never Fails (truck)
36. God Is Able International
37. God's Will Coke-a-Cola
38. Nothing but the Blood Barber Shop
39. Calvary Blood Tonic
40. Zion Car Wash Shop
41. My Dawn Restaurant
42. Father Into Thy Hands I Commit My Spirit (truck)
43. Who Is Free Fashions
44. Victory Electrical Works
45. Father Abraham Construction, Ltd.
46. Heavenly Fashion and Bridal Design
47. Savior Plumbing Works
48. Dr. Jesus Bread Stand
49. Follow Me to Jesus (truck)
50. God First Beauty Shop
51. God Never Fails Building Supply
52. Peace and Love Electrical
53. New Generation Plumbing

54. Clap for Jesus Coke-a-Cola
55. Heaven's Snacks
56. Almighty Plywood and Nails
57. Christ Is My Redeemer Beauty Shop
58. Have Faith Drug Store
59. Providence (business)
60. God Is Good Hair Cuts

Ain't these names outlandish? What if this caught on in America? What if Burger King changed its name to "The Lord's Supper Burgers"? What if the Hyatt changed its name to the "Heavenly Rest with Jesus Hotel"? Imagine an automatic door or gate company called "The Pearly Gates Are Open Door Company." What if a home builder named his company "You've Got a Mansion Just Over the Hilltop"? Would we think they were a little bit nuts? Probably.

But we may need to ask ourselves, *What's in a name?* I named my company "A Woman of God Ministries." I actually felt a little embarrassed using that name. I considered how people might view me. Would they think I'm self-righteous? Think about it: What if someone handed you a business card that said, "A Woman of God." Would you question her intent?

For a time I did struggle with that name for fear of being misunderstood, but I finally accepted it as a gift. Let me explain . . .

In early October 1995, at the insistence of my daughter Vikki, we went to visit a local television station to investigate the possibility of producing a Christian television program. While we were there, things happened very fast and I found myself signing a year's contract to produce a program that I had no name or format for and no experience producing. The station manager's assistant, Paulette, escorted us into the studio, and there we started praying. Soon, during our prayer, Paulette said, "Sister Thelma, the Lord says your program shall be called 'A Woman of God' because your mission is to represent God to women throughout the world. Since you have been faithful and a model of what a woman of God should be, your ministry will be a living example of a virtuous woman. Be proud to name your program, 'A Woman of God Ministries.'"

Wow! When she got through speaking, there was nothing else for me to do but accept the direction of God. Now I'm grateful to God for allowing me the privilege of being called a woman of God. I'm humbled by how God has used this name to encourage others to know him personally. And I'm not ashamed anymore.

In Ghana, I witnessed the great faith of the Christian natives, their bold love for Jesus, and how they were unashamed to proclaim him as Lord. They proclaim the name of Jesus in writing in everything they do. In the expression of his holy name they find solace and hope.

Outlandish as these commercial expressions may be, we Americans ought to be so bold. Remember the apostle Paul's words: "I am not ashamed of the gospel, because it is the power of God for the salvation of everyone who believes" (Romans 1:16).

> "If we want to be witnesses like Jesus, our only concern should be to be as alive with the love of God as Jesus was."
>
> —HENRI NOUWEN

God's Greatest Compliments

~ Luci Swindoll

I was lying in bed early this morning when I thought of a way to begin this devotional. For several weeks I've been writing, trying to finish my chapters, so just as I awakened I asked the Lord to help me be creative. Then it hit me. How 'bout this for an opening paragraph?

"Draw, you lily-livered, life-suckin' maggot," she said as she faced her opponent at the far end of the bar. "If you think you're leavin' this town with my man, you're crazy. I said—DRAW."

Ummm . . . okay. That's different. Eye-catching. A creative way to start a Christian devotional. *Are you sure, Lord? Did I hear that right?* I wasn't sure where the storyline would go from there, but I tore out of bed, raced to the computer, booted up, and started writing. Soon I realized that this was a fresh, fun answer to my prayer . . . a great way to begin the day.

A little while later, with a smile on my face and spring in my step, I marched triumphantly into the kitchen, put on the coffee, and something equally refreshing happened. I looked at the *Joyful Journey* flip calendar on my counter, and it so happened that the quote for the day was something I had written:

Find a new way to greet the day. Try a new way to drive to work—even if it's longer. Don't let the beaten path you travel daily beat you down too.

Oh my. How many times I've asked God for something specific, and he's dropped it in my lap; but because it didn't look like what I thought it should, I turned it down. *Forget that, Lord*, I say. *You've gotta be kidding.* God doesn't kid. He's the master of creativity, if I just trust him on that. So this morning I'm back at the drawing board, and I'm gonna *draw*.

I've discovered that life is so much easier when I take everything as a compliment from God. Every innovative idea, every unexpected circumstance, every outlandish twist along my path. The compliments I'm referring to are wrapped up in the mystery of becoming seasoned in the Lord as we grow more intimately acquainted with him, as we learn to see and hear past what is happening on the surface of our lives.

I learned this lesson the hard way. In 1982 I wrote my first book and was out of my head with joy about being The New Author on the block. I wrote constantly, talked about my writing, read chapters to everybody who slowed down long enough to listen, discussed ideas for the book with my editor and friends, traveled to the publishing house to meet the staff, kept a notebook about the progress I made. In short, I became a royal pain in the neck.

One day as I was waxing on and on with one of my dear friends, she lovingly told me that I was becoming a bore with all this book stuff. I was dominating dinner parties and weekends and was totally self-absorbed. Nobody else had the courage to point this out, but to save me from myself, she did.

I hated that revelation. It hurt me to hear those truthful words from a person I so loved. But, as I reasoned through her comments in the days ahead, I realized she was absolutely right. Then I wanted to retreat and never see those other friends again, I was so embarrassed by my self-centered behavior.

But as the weeks and months passed, and as I prayed about how I'd behaved and how to change, the Lord showed me something very helpful in James 1:2–5 (TLB). I had read it before, but that day it stuck.

> Is your life full of difficulties and temptations? Then be happy, for when the way is rough, your patience has a chance to grow. So let it grow, and don't try to squirm out of your problems. For when your patience is finally in full bloom, then you will be ready for anything, strong in character, full and complete. If you want to know what God wants you to

do, ask him, and he will gladly tell you, for he is always ready to give a bountiful supply of wisdom to all who ask him.

You see, *nothing* in our lives is wasted. Not one thing that happens is without worth somewhere down the road. But we often miss it because we "travel the beaten path" and fail to open our eyes to the outlandish ways God wants to speak to us and love us and change us. We don't recognize the value in celebrating the strange twists, the difficulties, the so-called failures, when we really should . . . and could. We consider our flops or hard times a defeat, but in reality they are God's greatest compliments. They're transforming love gifts from a gracious heavenly Father.

There's an account of this very point in *Say Please, Say Thank You* by Donald McCullough. The Ora-Ida frozen potato company celebrates anniversaries of failure. (They're the folks who make frozen cauliflower, broccoli, mushrooms, French fries, etc., and they're famous for innovative, creative ideas.) But what do they do when one of those ideas bombs? Do they blame or fire somebody? No, they throw a party! Literally. A cannon is fired and everybody stops work to commemorate the "perfect failure." Together they rejoice in what they've learned. They talk about what will not work, reveling in the fact that no more time, energy, or money has to be spent on a thankless project. They "celebrate their freedom to go on."

I'm not advocating a Pollyanna approach to life. That's totally unrealistic. We all go through terrible times of anxiety and loss— very real pain that takes time to go away, if it ever does. But there's a big difference between that and crawling under the house when things don't go our way or when our path takes what appears to be a too-outlandish turn.

If you wake up tomorrow with a thought that seems just a little bit crazy, or if a loved one brings your ego down to earth with a thud, take heart. It's God's complimentary gift to remind you who's in charge, who gives you freedom to go on . . . and who loves you with an outlandish love.

"Of all powers, love is the most powerful because it alone can conquer that final and most impregnable stronghold which is the human heart."

—FREDERICK BUECHNER

Diamond Dust

~ Barbara Johnson

A man was walking down the street when he passed a jewelry store. He stopped to admire some of the lovely pieces when he noticed the jeweler was preparing some stones. He watched him take uncut diamonds, which are yellow and quite unattractive, and place them in a machine. When they came out of the process the machine put them through, they were perfect, priceless diamonds.

This intrigued the man, and he entered the shop to inquire about this "magical" machine. The jeweler replied, "No, it's not the machine that works the 'magic,' it's what's *in* the machine: diamond dust. Only diamond dust can remove the ugly outer film of each uncut stone to allow the gem's brilliance to shine through."

When I heard that outlandish little story, I was transported back to a walk Bill and I took on the beach with some friends who own a cabin on the rugged coast of Maine. As we strolled along the shore, instead of fine sand we saw stones the size of tennis balls and others as large as basketballs. Yet they were all nearly perfectly rounded and smooth. The waves of the wild sea had transformed the once-jagged rocks into fine objects of beauty and wonder.

God works his outlandish "magic" on us in a similar way. Through the storms of life he transforms us into folks who are shaped in the likeness of his Son, who reflect his glory and shine like the precious gems he knows lie beneath what is unattractive in our appearance and behavior. We may wish for life's seas to be calm so we can live undisturbed, but God loves us too much to simply "leave us alone." When he sees our rough edges, he acts to remove them so we can become and enjoy exactly who we were created to be: his precious, beautiful jewels.

I know that if you're being tossed in the surf of life right now, these words can sound hollow rather than helpful. But that's why God has given us each other as we endure the storms of life: so we can "borrow" from each other's spiritual bank accounts of experience, hope, and faith when we're running low ourselves. Please, feel free to borrow from me! And from the many people who have walked the rocky shore before us.

The apostle Paul told us to "be joyful in hope, patient in affliction, faithful in prayer" (Romans 12:12). Sometimes the only way to do that is to simply "set our jaw" and continue trusting that God *is* here helping us, molding us, working his magic, despite what seems scary or bizarre about the process. When we put ourselves under his care, trusting that nothing can come into our lives except through his filter of perfect love and wisdom, then we *can* be joyful, hopeful, faithful . . . and ultimately transformed.

Does that mean we'll have no whirlwind emotions through all of this? Of course not. Human beings naturally get scared, angry, even ugly when they don't have control of what's going on in their lives. Even the most spiritually mature don't say, "Whatever, Lord!" without a few glitches now and then. But God can handle our thrashing about in fear and frustration, our crazy behavior when we don't get our way, even our fury at him when we're in pain and asking, *why?*

Madeleine L'Engle tells the story of one of her children when he was a toddler. "[He] used to rush at me when he had been naughty," she says, "and beat against me, and what he wanted by this monstrous behavior was an affirmation of love. And I would put my arms around him and hold him very tight until the dragon was gone and the loving small boy was returned. So God does with me. I strike against him in pain and fear and he holds me under the shadow of his wings."

That little snapshot of the infinitely loving, patient, compassionate, protective God of ours encourages me to take my "dragony" self straight into his presence when I am the most afraid and, therefore, the most in need of love. As Paul says in Hebrews 4:15–16, "For we do not have a high priest who is unable to sympathize with our weaknesses, but we have one who has been tempted in every way, just as we are—yet was without sin. Let us then approach the throne of grace with confidence, so that we may receive mercy and find grace to help us in our time of need."

So if you're going through a stormy time in your life, realize with gratitude that our all-wise, loving Father hasn't deserted you. He isn't allowing you to be tossed about like those rocks on the shore of Maine for no reason. He is working with awesome skill to smooth your rough edges and bring forth from your soul the brilliant loveliness of Christ, "so that you may be overjoyed when his glory is revealed" (1 Peter 4:13).

And meanwhile, the doors to his throne room are wide open to you. You can run to him any time, even beat on his chest in fear and fury, and he will hold you close until the dragon is gone and the lovely woman returns. He will sprinkle you with diamond dust until you sparkle with his loveliness. Now that's outlandish!

Joy is not the absence
of suffering but the
presence of God.

Moving On

~ Patsy Clairmont

Okay, okay, one more grandma story, then I'll stop . . . for a little while. I can't help myself. I'm so smitten with this darling boy. I knew it would be cool to be a grandparent, but I didn't realize how deep and significant it would feel.

So here's the story: When my daughter-in-law, Danya, was taken into surgery for a C-section, our little one stunned the doctor with his outlandish birth. When the incision was made, Justin slipped out his hand as if to greet the world, but when the doctor reached for it, Justin pulled his hand back inside his mommy's tummy and headed north. By the time the doctor finally caught him, she had to bring Justin into this world bottom side up, which she said was a first for her—a breech C-section!

Now, my take on this is that Justin was comfortable and felt safe right where he was. He appreciated being tucked close to his mom's heart and had no desire to have things change.

I know how that feels, and I bet you do too. Just when you have all your pillows fluffed and you have cozied in under the comforter, the doorbell buzzes, the telephone jingles, or the smoke detector squeals.

Recently I realized that I was going to add to my long saga of wandering (moving repeatedly). The home we live in now is unsuitable for my husband's growing disabilities, which is a legitimate need; but I confess I'm finding it difficult to change addresses again. I have loved this home, with all its nooks and crannies and lovely walking gardens. The cove ceilings and wide woodwork suit my love of antiques and my appreciation of history, and the small rooms have lent themselves to my enjoyment of cozy spaces. The location, too, has been a pleasure. Within minutes we can walk to town or stroll to the farmer's market on the weekends.

Yet I want, of course, what is best for Les. And I know that a year from now, I will take delight in our new home's special features: open floor plan, generous kitchen, and lovely view. For now, though, I'm wanting, like Justin, to scramble into the nearest hiding place and take refuge. But then I think about Justin's outrageous birth and, well, I just don't think I'd do "breech" well. I'm too old, and all that blood rushing to my head would leave me dizzier than I already am.

I wonder—it dizzies me to even imagine—how Christ brought himself to leave the security and purity of heaven to join us here on this sin-polluted planet. Talk about an outlandish birth! God himself born from a woman in a dirty barn. I wonder if Jesus was inclined to skedaddle back into the safety of his mom's womb when the time came for him to become God incarnate.

And talk about giving up an ideal location before he was conceived . . . From what I've heard, it doesn't get any better than Glory. The views in heaven . . . well, we can only imagine. I have yet to see a street of gold, a rainbow of emerald, a wall of jasper, or a pearl gate. And can you conjure up in your mind what heavenly music might sound like? I try, but I know my efforts fall short. The best I can do is Handel's *Messiah* on surround sound.

In Philippians 2 a melody rings for our souls. Listen in: "Your attitude should be the same as that of Christ Jesus: Who, being in very nature God, did not consider equality with God something to be grasped, but made himself nothing, taking the very nature of a servant. . . . He humbled himself and became obedient to death—even death on a cross!" (vv. 5–8).

Because of what Christ did willingly for us, we then can and should walk, skip, and run willingly toward embracing his servant attitude. That thought causes me to ask myself, "What's giving up a house on this sod anyway?" One day I'll have a mansion. Hallelujah!

I've decided little Justin reached out his hand to test the weather. Dear grandson, fear not! There is One who will starlight your darkest night and see you through till Glory.

"We got a home in Gloryland
that outshines the sun."
Now, that's a move I'm
looking forward to!

Intentional Love

My Friends,

Let me tuck in your pocket ten suggestions for finding happiness and wisdom and richness in your soul. These are things I've been learning for six decades, and they continue to be important to me.

Take God at his Word.

Do more than what is required.

Let the people you love know it.

Don't take yourself too seriously.

Never stop growing.

Own your own mistakes.

Enjoy what you have . . . it's all a gift.

See the beauty around you.

Live fully in this moment.

Study God's Word . . . it is life-giving.

When we live intentionally, loving intentionally follows suit, does it not? There's no way to escape it because we become proactive about everything. By his death on the cross Jesus gave us not only eternal life but abundant life as well. In other words, he gave us the capacity and the liberty to enjoy his unsparing generosity. What a gift . . . to have the God-instilled potential to love with intention, consideration, and forethought. Loving like that is so wonderful. It makes life full and fun. God, in his extravagant grace, reaches us through his boundless love . . . and knowing that for sure is best of all.

Loving you on purpose,

Swindoll

William the Rooster

~ Sheila Walsh

I t's three o'clock on a sticky summer's day in Charleston, South Carolina. If you drive slowly down Martello Drive you will meet some of the neighbors. In one yard, children are shouting and splashing in an inflatable pool. The two-year-old's diaper is hanging so low he looks like a budding rap artist. The couple next door are sitting in their white wicker rockers on the porch. The husband is fast asleep with the morning paper over his face. His wife is watching all the comings and goings of her small community.

Is she going shopping again?

When are they going to move that bus out of their yard?

Well . . . that's a brand new car!

I think I'll fix red beans and rice for supper. If I make enough, it should last two or three days.

I still can't believe they're letting that Alcoholics Anonymous group meet in our church. What next! Why, our old pastor would just turn over in his grave if he knew what was going on in the name of the Lord.

Farther down the street, an old man sits inside, alone, with a small oscillating fan pointed toward his lumpy old easy chair. He is trying to move the sticky air around his desolate life. He doesn't bother with the air conditioning. Doesn't seem worth it now that she is gone. In fact, he doesn't bother with much of anything anymore. Some days pass without a single meal. He finds himself dialing wrong numbers just to hear another human voice. He's not quite sure what day it is today, but he knows that by next Monday he'd better be on the ball when Social Services come to evaluate his competence to continue living alone. When the merciless sun sets tonight, he will slip out his back door and walk the half-mile to the cemetery. He'll sit under the outstretched limbs of a willow tree covered with Spanish moss. He likes to think it's her arms around him again.

A small boy is walking down the street. He must be nine or ten, slim with blond hair—a summer cut, close on his neck. He has on a blue T-shirt, long khaki shorts, and brown scuffed sandals. He is concentrating on kicking a shell dropped by a careless seagull. He is oblivious to the drama that is taking place behind the hedges as he passes by.

As an onlooker, it would be tough at first to identify the strange object that keeps popping up from behind the hedges and disappearing just as quickly. Is it a rooster? A small dog, perhaps? No, it's William Otto Pfaehler, the boy's father. His friends and family lovingly call him "The Rooster," but he's human all right. He's a dad. He's a protective, fiercely loving, and intentionally present father. And now he's my father-in-law, my own boy's grandfather.

William and Eleanor waited ten long years before they were gifted with their one-and-only child. When Barry arrived he was greeted with all the love and gratitude that eager parents can offer. He was like spring rain after a long drought. William wasn't about to let anything happen to this boy. So, on Saturdays when Barry walked past the few houses on his street to visit his godmother, Caroline, William took up his rooster position.

William knew that Barry wanted to be treated like a "big boy." He honored that, but in his own way. He would say, "Bye now, son! Have fun. Be a good boy for your Aunt Caroline." Then as soon as Barry was one house away, he'd dash out the front door and crawl along the grass behind the small neat hedges in each yard. Every few feet he'd pop his head up to make sure Barry was still there, that he hadn't been sold into white slavery or crushed beneath the hooves of marauding cattle.

We laugh about it now that William is eighty-one years old and lives with us. It seems once a rooster, always a rooster. I see him watching Christian with attentive intention, head bobbing up and down, lovingly guarding his only grandchild the way he watched over his only son.

Do you know that's just how God is with you? David the psalmist had a keen appreciation for the tender intentionality God has in never taking his eyes off his beloved children.

> The LORD watches over you—
> the LORD is your shade at your right hand;
> the sun will not harm you by day,
> nor the moon by night.
> The LORD will keep you from all harm—
> he will watch over your life;
> the LORD will watch over your coming and going
> both now and forevermore.
>
> —*Psalm 121:5–8*

God delights in the children that laugh and splash in the pool on a summer's day. He sees and loves the couple in the wicker rockers, even though his beloved busybody has missed the whole point that the church is just the right place for recovering alcoholics, and all the rest of us struggling through this life. God's heart aches for the man who sits alone watching his life tick away, and he wraps his arms around him under a willow tree with Spanish moss. He sees William and his son and *his* son.

Our outlandish, fearless, stubborn God watches over every single one of us. With tender parental attention. With perfect sovereign intention. That's just the kind of dad he is.

You have a tenacious,
intentional God who never,
ever lets you out of his sight.
He is there, always there,
watching lovingly over you.

Take Me Out to the Ball Game

~ Patsy Clairmont

When I was a youngster, I loved Saturday mornings. I would rise early without parental prompting, slide into my jeans and sweatshirt, gobble down a bowl of Snap, Crackle, and Pop dappled with sliced bananas, and head out the door to join my neighborhood friends. Almost always the boys, who happened to form the majority on the block, would decide to play baseball.

I loved competitive sports, except for one aspect—the process of choosing up sides. Being in the minority, I always was the choosee rather than the chooser. And no self-respecting boy would pick a girl until all the boys were divvied out. That was an unwritten code.

I found these intentional slights at best degrading and at worst humiliating. No, I wasn't a great player, but I was, as my kinfolk would say, dad-burn better than some of the fellows who were picked afore me.

Intentional is not "Oops, I didn't mean to do that" but "Here, take that." It's a deliberate decision. And nothing is more demeaning than to know you weren't considered up to par, you couldn't make the cut, and you were a deliberate reject.

On the other hand (I'm grateful there is another hand), when I hit high school and played in girls' organized sports, I frequently was chosen—and may I point out intentionally—usually among the first. *Y-e-s!* There is nothing like knowing you are preferred, esteemed, appreciated, applauded, and sought after. Although, sometimes we might wish to remain anonymous—like when the softball game turns to hardball . . .

Gideon was a man filled with fears and unanswered questions when suddenly, in the midst of his hardships, an angel of the Lord asked him to step up to the plate. Certain there had been a mistake, Gideon began to explain to the angel his error.

You see, Israel had been disobedient to the Lord so God had allowed the Midianites to shut out his people. The land was stripped of its crops and animals, and the Israelites, who had taken to the hills, resorted to hiding in caves. More enemies were swarming the land than fans attending the World Series.

And now this angel was asking Gideon to be the captain of God's team and to lead his people into the championship circle. Gideon tried to negotiate with the messenger by highlighting his own deficiencies. First he confessed to the heavenly scout his weak heritage, and then Gideon admitted he was the youngest in his family—why, he was just a kid!

When those tactics failed to dissuade the recruiter, Gideon asked for a divine sign (as if a visit from an angel wasn't a billboard statement). The Lord graciously accommodated Captain Gideon's faltering faith; yet even after the Lord gave Gideon a clear sign, he requested a repeat performance. I mean, this guy just couldn't believe the Lord had *intentionally* selected him.

As I read Gideon's story, I want to yell, "Excuse me, Gid, but the Lord chooses you on purpose! He knows your family history, your age, even your reluctance, and he still prefers you to all others. So what's your problem?"

Actually, even as I ask that of Gideon, the impact of it hits home with me. Truth be known, I too have those times in my life when I can't believe the Lord would choose *me*. Why, I can name off a teamload of others who are far better qualified, who have more impressive credentials, and who haven't struck out in their lives as consistently as I have. And yet he chooses me. How humbling for me. How gracious of him.

To know that God has a plan and we fit into it is proof enough to me of his intentional love.

Lord, thank you that you don't
keep track of our strikeouts
or even our homeruns. Instead,
you simply and graciously ask
us to step up to the plate.
To be on your team. Wow!

The Road to Hana

~ Barbara Johnson

I heard a story about a traveling executive who phoned his wife from an airport telephone, concluded their conversation with a hasty good-bye, and replaced the receiver. Just as he turned to walk away toward the boarding area, the phone rang. *Uh-oh*, he thought, *probably the operator calling back to tell me I talked longer than I paid for.*

He grabbed up the phone, and indeed it *was* the operator. But instead of asking for more coins she said, "Sir, I just thought you'd like to know . . . right after you hung up, your wife said she loves you."

Makes me stop and ponder . . . How many times do I miss out on God's blessings, designed especially for me, because I'm simply not "present," too much in a hurry, or looking way ahead instead of close by?

Last year my husband and I were in Maui. We'd heard so much about the great road to Hana. "Be sure to make that trip," people told us. And as Bill and I drove around the island, we noticed T-shirts and bumper stickers that proclaimed, "I survived the road to Hana." Well, being tourists and doing all the right touristy things, we hopped into an open jeep with some friends and set out for Hana. We just knew it had to be a great place to end up, and we rode along with high hopes.

The road is long, winding, and narrow. There are lots of turnouts; we noticed pretty little spots with waterfalls and creeks as we zoomed past. We didn't have time to stop or look at anything, though, because we wanted so badly to *get to Hana*.

Well, we finally made it. We clambered out of the jeep with great anticipation . . . and got the shock of our lives. There were no waterfalls or sparkling streams. No cute little restaurants. No town. Just a few palm trees and a gas station. There was nothing to see in Hana.

Chagrined, we realized that the *road* to Hana is what we were supposed to be enjoying. All the little turnouts we'd roared past were where the treasures awaited us. We'd missed them all in our hot pursuit of our destination. Fortunately, there was only one way down the windy road, so we got to see all we'd missed as we flew by the first time.

Sometimes I feel like my life is the road to Hana. I am so busy trying to get to the end that I miss many of the little turnouts. Unfortunately, in real life I can't go back the way I came and see what I missed.

What might you be missing today? Right now, I encourage you to stop the "car" of your life wherever you are and take a good look around you. And *listen*. Is someone trying to get you a message? *I love you* is certainly one you don't want to miss! *I need you* is one you dare not miss, especially if you have a teenager in the house! *"I am come that they might have life, and that they might have it more abundantly"* (John 10:10 KJV). Jesus didn't say that just to hear himself talk; he means it! His lavish, intentional love is for *me*, for *you*. Right now, and forever.

Since that day in the jeep I've tried to pay a lot more attention to my journey rather than my destination. After all, I *know* where I'm going! Even though my limited human imagination can't begin to fathom Glory, Christ promises that I am sure to arrive. No need to hurry. I know that heaven will be far better than Hana could ever be, but right now I'm *here*, not *there*. So I am trying to really *see* the waterfalls and hidden treasures all around me, to *hear* the love messages God intentionally leaves for me as I follow the road toward Home. He has filled my journey with splashes of joy on a daily basis, if only I have eyes to see, ears to hear, and a heart willing to *stop* and say, "Thank you."

God has two dwelling places:
one in heaven and the other
in a thankful heart.

Plotting for Love

~ Luci Swindoll

In the early spring of 1966 I went to Berlin for the first time. What an amazing, beautiful city! Even though it was marked by mounds of rubble and devastation from World War II, there were many things I remember with love: the Dahlem Museum, Charlottenberg Palace, Kennedy Platz, Kongress Hall, the Kurfurstendamm Strasse, the Kaiser Wilhelm church. One could easily see the architectural beauty that was once the glory of Germany.

At the time I was traveling with a friend whose relatives lived there, and we had the good fortune to be guests in their home. They introduced their friends and treated us like queens.

I recall an experience during the last afternoon of our visit that touched me deeply. We were riding in their car as they pointed out various spots of interest: buildings, monuments, streets, churches, stores. We drove through a neighborhood of modest homes, all built by hand after the bombings. Attached to every dwelling was a tiny plot of ground, beautifully manicured and full of green plants. None of the plots could have been larger than forty square feet. I asked about them.

"Those are love plots," I was told. "After the war, each person who built here received one as part of their property. Everybody who owns a house cultivates that plot of ground however they want. Some plant trees, others flowers or vegetables. We call them 'love plots' because the soil is tilled not only with labor ... but with love."

These lush little plots of ground struck me as more beautiful than any magnificent work of architecture I had seen. We were further told that the citizens of West Berlin were so devastated after the war that cultivating these tiny plots helped them come back to the center of what was important in their lives. They could plow and dig and hack and sow and plant and harvest to give life not only to what they were growing in the ground, but to their souls as well. Somehow those forty-square-foot plots gave a sense of sanity and homeostasis to the people who had lost so much in the war. It gave them a start. A new beginning. A purpose.

Life is like that at times. We are overwhelmed by someone who has hurt us, smeared our name, slandered our reputation. We feel there is never going to be even the smallest spot in our heart where there can be a new beginning. But the human spirit is resilient. After the destruction and anguish, eventually there is some small movement within us toward rebuilding. There is the first outcropping of creative energy and advancement toward recovery.

It starts slowly, a small flicker of light in the darkness, just enough to illumine what is eating us up inside. We open our hearts a crack, the light comes in, and change begins. It rarely commences with one major, gargantuan leap. As C. S. Lewis says in *Mere Christianity*, "If we really want to learn how to forgive, perhaps we had better start with something easier than the Gestapo."

Don't set your aim too high. Start with just "forty square feet," cultivating and overturning one lifeless clod of ground at a time. Through slowly and intentionally tending our inner landscape, we find that God's power flows in to change and soften our spirit. In time we realize that the thing we hate, that which has been paralyzing us, is usually our own fear or pride rather than an external enemy.

I well remember an occasion in my own life when there was a breach in one of my relationships. So much bitterness had lodged in my heart that I thought the feeling of betrayal would never go away. In the words of Marilyn's grandson, I was "boilin' mad" inside and had even thought of revenge. But time passed, and I got sick of myself living in the darkness of that animosity. I began to pray, first tentatively, then with solid intention, about the burden I was carrying and the person who had hurt me.

Little by little the surface of my packed-down feelings cracked open. A shaft of light got in and illumined and brought to life a seed of hope. Eventually I picked up the phone and talked to the individual by whom I felt betrayed. I purposefully reached out, and healing and growth began.

I've learned that as I bury the pain of hatred, I am planting the seeds of forgiveness. Working with actual dirt in my garden somehow helps me concentrate on what is simple and basic. Essential. The Source of life is there in my hands. All I have to do is put the seed in the ground and growth starts.

The same is true of the human heart. Change doesn't begin until I *do* something to start it. With that modicum of movement in the right direction, the Lord shines his warm light on the hard ground of my heart, and it softens. The writer of the letter to the Hebrews says, "Work at getting along with each other and with God. Otherwise you'll never get so much as a glimpse of God. Make sure no one gets left out of God's generosity. Keep a sharp eye out for weeds of bitter discontent. A thistle or two gone to seed can ruin a whole garden in no time" (Hebrews 12:14–15 MSG).

When our lives have been broken in battle and embittered by betrayal, the only place to start getting better is with a small plot. Inch by inch the soil of our heart is tilled and pruned by the Savior. It is beyond human reasoning or power to forgive someone who took everything we had and reduced us to rubble. But God, *but GOD,* in his boundless love, will meet us right in that very place and start planting the seeds of hope and peace and strength and forgiveness . . . and we will come to life again. In the words of Henri Nouwen, "Love is an act of forgiveness in which evil is converted to good and destruction into creation."

The Berliners gave beauty to that which was ugly. They toiled together making gardens of green from mounds of rubble and ruin. Nobody said it was easy, but everybody said it was worth it.

Do some digging in the soil of your heart and see what turns up. Make up your mind to let God plant some new seeds in the "plot" of your soul. And then grow.

The Ultimate Power Source

~ Marilyn Meberg

Yesterday, in the midst of one of my mindless thinks, I startled myself with a thought. Because my mind had been formless and void, it was a notable moment. Interestingly enough the thought was not new, but it came with such intensity it had the feel of new. It was this: *greater power is available to all God's people.*

Well . . . since I am one of God's people, I had to personalize that thought. I certainly recognized my frequent sense of powerlessness, so the prospect of greater power was compelling. If more power is available, how do I get it?

The metaphor that came to me was that of an electrical outlet. When I need power for anything (my wild boar meat strainer or vegetable puree-mash mixer) I plug in. Simple. So am I not "plugged in" to God's power? After all, I'm a Christian . . . I study my Bible . . . I pray. Do I need bigger plugs? What am I missing?

Let me seemingly go down a rabbit trail and tell you an experience I had with my golf cart. To begin with, I adore my golf cart. My schedule keeps me off the golf course (which ensures the physical well-being of all within range of my unpredictably wild and erratic shots), but the cart is my mode of transportation around the condominium complex in which I live. My neighbors and I toodle to each other's homes via our respective golf carts . . . never a car.

One balmy late afternoon I called my neighbor Luci and asked her to join me in my cart for a quick beyond-our-gates trip to the pharmacy.

"Is your cart street-legal, Marilyn? Are you supposed to drive it on public roads?"

"No . . . but we aren't going far, and we'll take the back streets."

Quickly convinced, Luci and I took off to pick up my hormones.

On the ride home I felt fully confident that my little cart was destined for every public thoroughfare in America. I breathed in the scent of citrus blossoms, reveled in my radio's reception of Vivaldi's "Four Seasons," and said to Luci, "In the words of some beer commercial, it doesn't get any better than this."

As she was about to agree, my cart did an unprecedented cough, and belch, skipped two heartbeats . . . and died. Not only did my cart die dead away, we were in the middle of a fairly busy intersection. With a squealing of brakes, several cars went careening off left and right in an attempt to avoid rear-ending us. As we breathlessly pushed her (my cart . . . I call her a "her" . . . actually, her name is Celeste) onto the sidewalk, I kept telling Luci, "She can't have a dead battery! Look, the lights are on and the radio's still doing Vivaldi. Not only that, she was plugged into the power charger for several hours this morning; she's been fully juiced!"

"Juice or no juice, Marilyn, how do you expect to get this fully-charged baby home?"

Grimly talking our way through as many unworkable plans as we could think of, I got the brilliant idea of calling AAA for emergency roadside assistance. After all, I was in a disabled vehicle by the side of the road. I'd been a club member for over thirty years and hardly ever called them. Now was the perfect time!

By now it was completely dark. Were it not for the intersection streetlights I'd never have been able to make out the emergency phone number on the back of my AAA card. Successfully punching in the number on Luci's cell phone, I tried to explain my predicament to the very, very young male who received my call. He commiserated with me about my breakdown, took my street location, and then asked for a description of my vehicle.

"Well . . . my vehicle is small . . . kind of convertible-like. It's turquoise with a tan top. And my name, Marilyn, is written in script letters on the left-hand side." After a long pause, the very, very young voice asked, "Ma'am . . . are you describing a car?"

"Uh no . . . I'm describing my disabled vehicle."

With absolutely no effort at self-control, he began to laugh and said it sounded as if I was describing a golf cart. When I owned up to that fact, he laughed even harder and told me that AAA did not "assist" golf carts.

"Well, how about a golf cart owner and her friend who are both very, very old and sitting on a sidewalk in the dark, unprotected in a bad neighborhood, with no hope of assistance or even defense should someone decide to prey on the elderly?" (Actually, it was not a bad neighborhood, but we were old and I knew Celeste was dangerously appealing.)

That plea seemed to spark a helpful spirit in the boy. He told me he'd give our location to a tow-truck company who would haul us home, but it would be at my expense. Forty-five minutes later, an enormous flatbed truck pulled up. After assuring the driver that my cart was indeed the vehicle to be hauled, Celeste was hoisted up with huge cable chains and placed in the middle of the truck, where she settled conspicuously with room for at least two Winnebagos on either side of her. Luci and I heaved our way up into the truck cab, which was at least thirty-one feet higher than the street surface, and with much commotion, including flashing lights, we made our way to my quiet, unsuspecting neighborhood, where Celeste deftly slid down the ramp into my garage.

The next morning the "cart doctor" made a house call. I learned that in spite of Celeste being fully charged from my conscientious "plug in," her battery wires had short-circuited, which produced a wire meltdown.

So, you must be wondering, *what in the world is this woman's point? What does all this have to do with that now-faraway thought during her mindless think?* Here's how it connects for me; see if it does for you as well.

The realization that God intends for each of us greater power than we are currently experiencing is tremendously encouraging. From his original intentionality, from before the foundation of the world, God intended for us to be power-based. That is, *Power*-based. Though we may be "plugged in" as it relates to salvation, prayer, and Bible study, sometimes we nevertheless short-circuit, lose power, and go dead in the middle of life's intersections. We don't lose our salvation; we don't lose his love. But we lose power.

So how do we get it back? More important, how do we hang onto it and not lose it in the first place? The answer lies in the use of the name Jesus. His name is the ultimate power source. The apostle Paul said in his letter to the Christians at Philippi: "God highly exalted Him, and bestowed on Him the name which is above every name, so that at the name of Jesus every knee will bow . . . every tongue will confess that Jesus Christ is Lord" (Philippians 2:9–11 NASB).

Scripture reminds us repeatedly of the power in that holy name and urges us to use it for our every need. Shortly before Jesus left the earth, he specifically advised his disciples on the use of his name, saying, "Until now you have asked for nothing in My name; ask, and you will receive, so that your joy may be made full" (John 16:24 NASB). Jesus pointed out to his followers that using his name in prayer was new, but from that moment on he intended that they would have constant access to a new power source . . . his name.

In my life's current intersection, I've realized anew that though I remain plugged in simply because my faithful God won't disconnect from me, my sense of powerlessness that comes and goes may lie simply in my forgetting or neglecting to use the Name. I may be too overwhelmed, tired, or sick to even present my needs to God. When that happens I can simply say the Name: Jesus . . . Jesus . . . Jesus. When there are no words, when there is no strength, there is always his Name.

There is no greater Power source, my friend. God's boundless love provides it; his intent is that we use it.

"My hope is built on nothing less
Than Jesus' blood and righteousness;
I dare not trust the sweetest frame,
But wholly lean on Jesus' name."

—EDWARD MOTE

Holy Spring Cleaning

~ Sheila Walsh

The alarm buzzed like an army of killer bees. I looked through a sleepy haze at the clock on my night stand. 6:45 A.M.

But this is Saturday! I thought, as I prepared to throw the clock through the window. *An evil force must have set it during the night.* I looked over at Barry, content in dreamland, and wondered if he was the evil force. And then I remembered. An army of worker ants would be here at 8:00 to refinish our hardwood floors.

We had been in our new house for only a couple of months. But every time I vacuumed or passed through the den I would end up on my knees trying to scrape bits of white paint off the dark wood. I couldn't get them to come off no matter how hard I tried. One day the builder was dropping off a missing piece for our refrigerator, and I asked him if he knew what the problem was.

"Oh sure!" he said. "We put a topcoat of varnish on the floors after the painters had finished painting, so it sealed all the paint in."

I stared at him for a moment, trying to process what he had said. I blundered on. "Wouldn't it have been a good idea to have removed the paint before you put the topcoat of varnish on?"

"Yes," he said jovially. "That would have been a great idea."

After he left, I sat for a while trying to work out which one of us was nuts. I decided it was him, so I called him.

"I don't like all the paint on the floor. This is a brand new house and it looks like it was finished by Laurel and Hardy." He laughed. He thought I was kidding. Big mistake! "No, seriously," I said as kindly as I could muster, "I'd really like you to get the paint off."

"But that will mean we'll have to move all your furniture and sand the floors again and then finish them again."

"Great plan!" I said. "Good-bye, Laurel."

And so the work crew arrived at 8:00 A.M. on Saturday. Christian and I hid upstairs in his playroom and watched *Alice in Wonderland.* When the floors were finished they were lovely and all one color, may God be praised! We replaced the furniture, put fresh flowers in a vase, and sat back and thanked God again for our home.

Then Barry had a wonderful idea. He called one of our church elders and asked him if he would come over and dedicate our home to the Lord. I'd never formally done that before, but I loved the thought. So Steve and Marilyn Lorenz and our good friend Cindy Wilt arrived one Friday night for the "service." We sat out on the deck and sang, "This is My Father's House." Then Steve read the passage from Ephesians on spiritual warfare: "For our struggle is not against flesh and blood, but against the rulers, against the authorities, against the powers of this dark world and against the spiritual forces of evil in the heavenly realms" (6:12).

"We have no authority ourselves," Steve reminded us. "But Christ has authority over all the powers and wickedness that surround us. So we will begin at the front of the house and pray room by room that there be no evil lurking in any corner. I will anoint every door and passageway with oil and pray for God's presence to be felt by all who enter here."

What followed was one of the most moving experiences of my life. We went into Christian's room and anointed his bed. We prayed in his playroom and over all his toys. We thanked God for William and asked for long life and health as Steve anointed the door of his bedroom. We came into my study where I write and pray. I knelt on the floor as Steve anointed my head with oil and asked God to use this earthen vessel as a channel of his grace and love. We moved to our bedroom and offered our marriage to the Lord again. Then Steve anointed Christian.

"What's that stuff you're putting on my head? It smells funny."

"It's oil, darling," I said. "Uncle Steve is going to pray for you."

"Cool!" Christian replied.

We went into the guest room and asked that God's presence would fill the room and that anyone who slept here would experience the peace and rest that is found only in Christ. In the yard we looked to the house on our right and on our left and prayed God's blessing on our neighbors.

After everyone had gone home and Christian was tucked in bed and fast asleep, I sat outside under the stars and a full silver moon. "Lord," I prayed, "thank you for tonight. Thank you for the richness of my life and my family. Just as we have prayed that there would be no dark corners in our home, I pray that there would be no dark corners in my heart. Sweep through every room with your presence and make me a place that you can live with joy. I see the paint spills in my soul and thank you that your blood, your perfect love, covers me. Thank you for your gracious, relentless, intentional love. Amen."

That is how each one of us is loved by God. It's no accident or random thing. God loves all of us and longs to fill our hearts and our homes with his fragrance. Perhaps today you might walk through your own home and your own heart and intentionally invite him to fill every crevice, corner, and empty space . . . "And so at last you will be filled up with God himself" (Ephesians 3:18).

God longs to fill you
to overflowing with his vibrant
life and his boundless love.
Let his fragrance fill
your heart and home.

Let's Have a Party!

~ Thelma Wells

I love a celebration! And every day at my great-grandparents' house was a celebration as I grew up under their tender care. They'd praise God for anything and everything. They held prayer meetings in our house. They would sing and pray and read the Scriptures with some of the people in our church and neighborhood. Sometimes these meetings would get so loud that I'd get embarrassed because I thought people outside could hear us. Nevertheless, I was right there in the middle with them, partying in the presence of the Lord!

In my world growing up, praise and worship were revered. You could walk into the sanctuary of our church and feel the presence of the Lord in a palpable way. As a young girl, I didn't know how to identify what that feeling was, but I felt a peacefulness come over me in church unlike in any other place. Sunday was so special to me. It was my favorite day of the week because it was a high, holy day of worship and praise for all of us.

People in our church would sing or pray or testify until they got "happy" and began shouting. That same joy still flows in some of our churches today. I remember being with author Anne Lamott when she described her church. She says that when she first started attending this primarily black church, the moans and groans of "amen" and outcries of "hallelujah" bothered her. She had not experienced emotions like that in church before. She thought of them as distractions to hearing the "real" message. But as she grew more accustomed to those sounds, she understood the genuine praise and worship they portrayed, and she grew to appreciate them. She remembers when one of the older men of the church died, and how much she missed his voice of thunderous praise—the holy sound of true worship.

Praise and worship doesn't only happen in church, of course. It can happen anywhere. As a little girl, I would sing all the time in the privacy of my great-grandparents' little back alley apartment. I would sing old hymns and choruses like "Nearer My God to Thee," "What a Friend We Have in Jesus," and "Jesus Loves Me, This I Know." I'd sing those songs and feel something swelling up in my spirit. I didn't know what it was, but my eyes would begin to fill up and tears would run down my round cheeks. This emotion, this exuberance, this *Presence* would overpower me. It was like a celebration in my heart. It was a party!

However, as I grew older and allowed life's challenges to encumber my childlike, praiseful spirit, I would wonder, *Why do I need to spend my precious time praising the Lord when I could be doing so many other things like speaking to groups, playing with my children, romancing my husband, or exploring new adventures?* Life certainly has a way of getting in the way sometimes! But I quickly noted that as I decreased my praise time, my joy also decreased. I found out that when I made a habit of intentionally giving God the praise he deserves, I appreciated life so much better.

Take a look outside. What do you see? Do you see blue skies, rainbows, moonlit nights, twinkling stars in a vast galaxy? Do you feel the summer breeze, the fat drops of spring rain, the soft icy snowflakes on your tongue? Can you smell the fragrance of the fresh-mown grass and budding flowers? Not one twig on a tree bends, not one petal falls from a flower, without God's permission. He made all and controls all in heaven and on earth. So we praise him because of the splendor, majesty, and glory of his creation. "Let them praise the name of the LORD, for his name alone is exalted; his splendor is above the earth and the heavens" (Psalm 148:13).

We also praise God because we are recipients of his mighty acts of salvation and redemption. When Adam and Eve disobeyed their Creator, the whole human race was lost in sin. Then God came down to earth in human flesh as Jesus and claimed us back to himself.

Jesus Christ died on a cruel, rugged cross to purchase our salvation through his blood. Those who have accepted him as Lord and Savior have been reclaimed as children of the Most High God! We have been saved from the ravages of sin. We are promised eternal life with God, the Creator; Jesus, his Son; and the Holy Spirit, our ever-present Comforter. Now that's a reason to praise him!

And not only have we been redeemed and saved by the blood of Jesus, but God also delivers us from everyday problems. He rescues us from situations that seem impossible. He often heals our sicknesses and diseases. He calms our anxious hearts. When we have problems, disappointments, and tough decisions to make, he reminds us through his Word that he is in control of it all. No sickness or disease, financial dilemma, loss of a loved one, addiction, distress, peril, disaster, danger, or anything else can ever separate us from his protection, guidance, and boundless love. Now that makes me shout, "Hallelujah!"

Finally, God causes us to prosper. God's gift of prosperity goes far beyond money or luxuries. His favor extends to all areas of our lives as he meets our physical, emotional, and spiritual needs. Many of our wants are provided as well because God showers us with his blessings. And I mean *all* of us. Each and every one. God doesn't love me any more than he loves you. I don't have a monopoly on God's love and grace. He has assured us all through his Word that he will keep us in perfect peace if we keep our minds on him (Isaiah 26:3).

Most of the time, as soon as my feet hit the floor in the morning, I turn on praise music. I love gospel music; it gets me going! In fact, when people enter my home, they will almost always hear music playing. There's something about listening to praise music that opens up the portals of heaven on earth and reassures me that I'm surrounded by God's loving presence.

My great-grandmother used to sing, "I woke up this morning with my mind stayed on Jesus." As a morning ritual my husband sings (in the shower), "I know the Lord will make a way! Oh yes, he will." I take music on the road with me when I travel. It's an integral part of my lifestyle, and I love it.

Sometimes I even dance! Now, I'm not a good dancer, but I can dance before the Lord. Sometimes I pretend to be Miriam and dance all over my house. The gospel artist Fred Hammond recorded a song that says, "When the Spirit of the Lord comes upon my heart, I will dance like David danced." Well, sometimes I'm dressed almost like David (barely clad), and I dance before the Lord with vigor and in reverence to his holy name.

Another way I praise God is to be silent before him. "But the Lord is in his holy temple. Let all the earth be silent before him" (Habakkuk 2:20). Sometimes it's hard just to be quiet. But Scripture says that it's in quietness and trust that we find our strength in the Lord (Isaiah 30:15). So why don't you try it for a minute? Take one minute just to be silent before the Lord. Then as you reflect on your life and how God has provided for you, stand up, raise your hands in praise, open your mouth, and shout, "Praise the Lord! Thank you, Father! You've been so good to me!"

What you'll discover as you intentionally give your heart to God in praise is that he will praise you back! In fact, Scripture says that God actually sings over us when we praise him. "He will rejoice over you in great gladness. . . . Is that a joyous choir I hear? No. It is the Lord himself exalting over you in happy song" (Zephaniah 3:17 TLB).

So, dear friend, whether you are surrounded by a huge crowd or resting in your bed, praise God in the morning, praise him in the noon day, praise him in the evening. Let everything that has breath praise the Lord!

God doesn't love me any more
than he loves you! Together,
let's praise his wonderful name.
It's time to *PARTY*!

Eek!

~ Patsy Clairmont

I can't imagine living in a culture in which, when the time came to be married, someone else (my parents, a matchmaker) picked out my husband. Why, what if he was a nerd? Eek!

I'm not just talking about a thick-lensed, high-water pants, straight-A-student kind of fellow. I wouldn't dare since I wear glasses (which have—ahem—thickened up over the years); I own several pairs of pants that I've shrunk in the dryer (Help! I shrunk my pants and my ankles are showing); and I took a night class recently in which I received an A for my efforts. *Oh, no, I'm a nerd.* Eek!

All kidding aside, selecting a husband is intimate business, and I don't want anyone to make the choice for me. Really now, what if they chose the wrong flavor?

As it is, my husband, Les, is Chunky Monkey, and I am Tutti-Frutti. Now, isn't that a lip-lickin' match? We think so. But who would have thought of that combo? Sounds like instant indigestion, yet it works for us. Well, *now* it does.

When I met Les, I was only fifteen, and he was sixteen. He immediately liked me, and I instantly disliked him. By the end of a week (what a difference a day makes when one's heart skips a beat), I was wild about him. I found Les was outrageously funny, sweetly romantic, and kind-hearted (which continues to be true).

We lived more than five hundred miles apart, which nixed dating for us. Instead, we saw each other sporadically for short visits, always in the company of others, until we married at the ripe old ages of seventeen and eighteen.

After we said, "I do," we found out "we don't." We were totally unprepared for facing real life together and even less prepared for loving each other intentionally. We were more into convenient love—when all was going well, and it was easy to love the other one. We discovered that intentional love was a lot of work, a big commitment, and the giving up of personal "rights." Eek!

It took us years of hurt feelings, bouts of sullenness, and many verbal volleys before we learned how to love purposefully. Still today we have to make up our minds to love each other when one of us is being obstinate, emotionally withdrawn, or lippy. It's easy to take on someone else's bad mood if we aren't cautious, and it's even easier to respond in anger when the other person acts ticked. When you have two hotheads in the house, it's like striking two matches: the obvious result is fire. The only way to keep things from sparking is for one partner to become water to douse the flames. Mature love, intentional love, holds steady until the other partner regains his or her footing.

Through the years Les and I have had many opportunities to acquiesce to each other: during those ill-explained monthly moments when the slightest provocation could set me off in a torrent of tears; or during those times when unemployment pressed down on Les's last nerve (I remember financial battles that made us both defensive); and after Les's heart surgery, which left him emotionally vulnerable for a while. And then we had to face my tug-of-war with depression. If Les hadn't intentionally chosen higher ground, we both could have taken the plunge (and I don't mean the Nestea plunge—aah!).

Intentional loving doesn't mean giving in, but giving up—giving up the ineffectual habit of responding in like negative manner to another. That's the human tendency, but it's not true love's tendency.

When Jesus walked the countryside, he demonstrated his determination to love us intentionally by overlooking slights, sidestepping fights, and giving up his rights. And nowhere do we see that more dramatically than when, on Calvary, Jesus cried out regarding his accusers and his abusers, "Father, forgive them, for they do not know what they are doing" (Luke 23:34). And he said that *before* the people ever regretted their decision to crucify him.

Jesus left for us definite love-markers—indelible, incredible, intentional. Our way isn't to tolerate an insult, back away from a bully, or yield our puny rights, which is why Jesus said, "I am the way" (John 14:16). Is he asking us to be cowering, quivering flunkies? Quite the contrary. He calls us to be courageous, single-minded servants who choose love. Intentionally.

"In the Christian sense, love is not primarily an emotion but an act of the will."

—FREDERICK BUECHNER

The Beautiful Boy
and the Seven Kings

~ Sheila Walsh

A Bedtime Tale for Christian and His Mommy . . .

Once upon a time in a land far, far away, there lived a beautiful boy. His name was Christian. Christian lived with Sheila his mommy, Barry his daddy, William his papa, Lily the cat, and a rather cross fish named Red. Christian was the most beautiful boy in the whole land.

One day there was a loud knock at the door and the sound of a trumpet. It was the royal trumpet, announcing the arrival of the king. Christian's daddy went to the door and invited the king to come into their home. The king sat in the green chair by the fire and invited the family to sit around him.

"We are so honored by your visit, your majesty," Barry said. "How may we serve you?"

"Well," the King replied. "More of that in a moment. First I am here to meet your son. I have been told that he is the most beautiful boy in our part of the world."

"That is true, your majesty," the mommy replied with a soft smile.

"Then may I meet him?"

William went to the playroom and called Christian's name. Soon the boy appeared. He was wearing green pants, a green sweater, a green ball cap, and rather magnificent green shoes.

"Christian, this is our king," William said.

The boy approached the king and bowed before him. The king looked at this fine young man and smiled.

"Yes, indeed. He is the most beautiful boy in the whole land."

The king began to explain the reason for his visit. "As you know, we live in a world with seven lands—seven kings govern seven kingdoms. It is my desire that you would board the royal ship and sail around to the other six kingdoms by sunset tomorrow. At the royal port of each land, the king will bring the most beautiful boy in his kingdom to meet with you. It will be decided by him alone which boy is the most beautiful."

With that, the king rose from his chair and bid them all farewell.

The next day, Barry, Sheila, William, and Lily packed for the trip. Barry packed six sweaters. Sheila packed six books. William packed six bars of chocolate. Lily packed six mice. Red packed nothing. She was far too cross about the trip. Even though she was a fish she did not like water at all, preferring to sit in a chair by the fire. Christian packed his six favorite toys.

By sunset they were all on board the royal ship. It was quite a magnificent vessel. It was painted in a striking shade of green and the sails were green and the mast was green too. Everyone stood on deck to watch the ship pull up anchor (except for Red, who was sulking in her cabin).

In the morning they reached the Blue Kingdom. The ruling king was there to meet them, and by his side there was a fine young boy. The two boarded the royal ship and shared some tea. When it was time to leave, the Blue king admitted to Barry, "Your son is the most beautiful boy I have ever met."

As the king and the boy left the ship Christian ran after them and gave the boy one of his six favorite toys. Then the royal ship sailed on.

They dropped anchor at the Purple Kingdom, and once more Christian was chosen as the most beautiful boy. At each port he left, one of his favorite toys was also left with the child who stayed behind.

When they came to the Red Kingdom, the most amazing thing happened. Even as the Red king was declaring Christian to be the most beautiful boy, Red, the very cross fish, was jumping up and down, which, as you know, is quite difficult for a fish.

"Whatever is the matter?" Barry asked.

"Look, it's red. All red! The trees are red, the sky is red, the water is red. I love red water!" With that she jumped overboard and swam away. It was a most unusual day.

Finally they reached the Silver Kingdom. As they began to approach the port, Lily the cat appeared on deck.

"Looks like you've lost here," she said. "Look at that boy standing beside the Silver king."

They all looked at the darling boy with pale silver hair, a silver coat, and sparkly silver shoes. He was quite beautiful. The Silver king and the boy came on board for some tea and cake. They talked and laughed for a long time, but finally they had to go as the silver sun was setting in the silver sea.

The Silver king spoke: "I never believed it would be possible to meet a boy more beautiful than this boy of mine, for you see, he is my son. But we both agree, Christian is the most beautiful boy in all the world."

Before the silver boy left, Christian gave him his last and very best toy.

By morning the royal ship had arrived home and the king was there to meet them. They told him all about their wonderful adventure.

"So you are the most beautiful boy in all the lands!" the king said with a smile.

"Thank you, your majesty," Christian said humbly before he and his mommy and daddy and William and Lily went home. Christian missed Red, even though she was always so cross.

That night, as Christian's mommy was tucking him into bed, she asked him if he had enjoyed his adventure.

"I did, Mommy. But it made me sad to watch the other boys walk away. I thought they were *all* beautiful."

"But that is why *you* are beautiful, darling," his mommy replied. "You are beautiful in your heart, and that is the fairest color of all."

That night, when Christian was fast asleep in his bed, his mommy knelt beside him and prayed: "Thank you, blessed King, for this boy. Thank you for his beautiful heart. Help us to raise him to love as you love. Thank you for sending your own most beautiful Boy to such a foreign land to change the color of our lives forever."

We are beautiful when we intentionally live and love as Christ does. Don't look at what you don't have; just open your eyes to who you are — and whose you are!

Keep Sending Out Love

~ Barbara Johnson

My son just doesn't call me the way he should. I'm lucky if I'm graced with a voice-mail once a month. Is it too much to ask to hear from my own son more often than that? I mean, I'm his *mother*, for Pete's sake." (I wonder who Pete is?)

This mom of a young man recently graduated from college and off into the big wide world sounded angry, but I knew she was hurting. I could see it in her eyes. *Doesn't he love me anymore?* I could hear her heart wondering. *Doesn't he recognize anything I've done for him? Doesn't he miss me like I miss him? Oh, how I miss him!*

Instead, out of her mouth came the petulant words, "Well, fine. I just won't call him back. I'm not chasing him down to get his attention. He can just see what it feels like to not hear from *me* for a long, long time. I'll give him some of his own medicine, see how he likes it." *Oh God, please let me hear from him! I miss him! I want my boy!*

Being a mother has its Hallmark card moments . . . and then it has its Far Side scenarios. Or worse. Someone has said, "Raising children is like being pecked to death by a chicken!" On those painful days, how tempting it can be to give up, retreat and pout, or even strike back. But as a mother, there is simply no place to resign. (I know the lady who wrote that book; she is nuts but also an authority on the subject.) So trust me . . . you might as well kick back and enjoy your life! If your kid is "out to lunch" and forgets you for days or weeks, find another lonely kid and use your imagination to bring love into his or her life instead. So what if you don't get a birthday card from your daughter on time, or even a call to let you know she's arrived safely when you've been praying the whole day she's been at the wheel? I know it hurts, but how you *respond* will make all the difference—both in your own heart and in your relationship with your child.

Next time you're nursing your mother wounds, try something different. Something intentionally loving. Call *her* to see how she's doing, even if you can hear her eyes roll over the phone. Send *him* a note telling *him* that you love him, even if you don't get anything warm and gooey in return. I know you want more; sometimes you just wish you could turn back the hands of time and hold him in your arms like a baby.

I wanted more too. But when two of my sons were killed and a third was estranged from me for over a decade, I had a hard choice to make. Would I just put my mother's heart on the shelf and determine to stop this "loving" business because it was simply too painful, too risky? Naturally, I was tempted! I felt more than "pecked" by raising and losing children so dear to me; I felt sliced open (without any anesthesia), gutted, and left for dead. But God is in the resurrection business. He didn't want the mother's heart he'd planted in me to be sidelined or sealed up, even though he knew I felt I had good reason to cash it in on sending out any more mother's love into the world.

So he gave me an opportunity to keep on giving. A blessing in thousands of different disguises. I got to love other people's kids. Other hurting parents. Other devastated moms. Why did God do this? Just to keep on pushing me to obey his commandment to love, even though I felt like I was running on empty? Is that the kind of God we have—one who insists on using us up for his purposes without any regard to how we feel?

Absolutely not! He wants us to keep sending out love because he knows that when we stop, our hearts wither and grow hard. The soil that he longs to keep tilling and planting till the day we die becomes packed down with sorrow and bitterness, and we miss the harvest of all he has yet to bring forth in our lives regardless of our heartaches and disappointments.

God is never finished using us, but he is also never finished blessing us! No matter how grave our losses in this sin-strewn land we're passing through on our way to Glory, God's loving intention is to fill our empty arms, heal our broken hearts, and "replant" our barren souls. He can't do that very abundantly if we close up shop on the loving business and hang our broken hearts on a hook somewhere in the back.

So do yourself a favor: Don't rob yourself (and don't let anyone else rob you either) of the abundance that belongs to you in Christ. Instead of giving up, keep giving out. Just keep sending out love. Keep planting and watering seeds. You may grow yourself a "blooming idiot," but don't stop being who God made you to be! Be glad for your mother's heart. Your love is special and powerful, like God's: "As a mother comforts her child, so will I comfort you" (Isaiah 66:13).

Let God's motherly love wrap around your bruised and battered heart and comfort you until you are ready to send out love again.

Love is the fairest flower
that blooms in God's garden.

The Fabric of Love

~ Luci Swindoll

You wonder why some women never marry? There are, of course, many reasons, but one is that they never find Mr. Perfect. *Where is he?* They are looking for a guy the height of John Wayne, with the build of Schwarzeneggar, the looks of Omar Shariff, the wit of Dick Cavett, and the know-how of McGyver. He's out there somewhere, they just *know* it. But where?

Edna St. Vincent Millay wrote a tongue-in-cheek poem called *To the Not Impossible Him* where she confesses there is no way to know for sure you've met the right man unless you consider a good many . . . unless you travel the world and test the waters. I'm sure there's some truth to that.

My mom and dad had an almost perfect love match. The year mother died they were just about to celebrate their fortieth wedding anniversary, and every year they were married was full of simple and intentional celebrations of their love and thoughtfulness to each other.

I was cleaning out a drawer a couple of mornings ago and ran across some of Mother's old jewelry; worthless stuff generally, but touching to me, nevertheless. In that batch of stuff was a compact with powder and rouge still in it, believe it or not. I saw it many times when I was growing up. Daddy gave it to her shortly after they married in 1931, and Mother told me he had mailed it from one of his trips with a note about how much he loved her. On the little powder puffs he'd printed in big letters—EARL—so she would see his name and think of his love every time she opened that compact.

I love it when couples and friends do that kind of thing for one another. It says so much about their love, and it's often treasured for life. Just think, my mother carried that compact until she died in

1971, and every time she opened it, there was her husband's name, saying "I love you."

If I didn't love the single life so much, I might be looking for Mr. Perfect too. In fact, the closest ideal I've ever met with respect to my first-paragraph dreamboat is my long-time friend Kurt Ratican. He's handsome, bright, well-read, terribly witty, clever, and exceedingly kind. He's not ... well ... *perfect*. But close. And he does the same types of things my father did for my mother. He sends his love to me in unique ways all the time.

Among Kurt's many artistic talents is weaving, and he taught me to weave on a tiny wooden loom that was a Christmas gift from him in 1969. Included with the loom was a guidebook called *Simple Weaving.* It's full of his notes of instruction and encouragement. When I look at it, I think back on the day he gave me the loom and the sweet kindness that followed.

Because we lived in different states at the time (he in California and I in Texas), he told me he would "dress" the loom the first time if I'd let him take it home after our Christmas celebrations together. I was a novice so was thrilled at the prospect of his doing the hardest work. I knew nothing about heddles, raddles, bobbins, drums, cranks, or shuttles, and he knew *everything*. (Actually I knew about cranks, but that's another story.) I was one happy girl.

Kurt owns a very large loom and has woven many beautiful things for me through the years; but nothing of his design or thoughtfulness could have pleased me more than what I saw when I opened the box he sent back to me after the holidays. There sat the completely dressed loom with a portion of a geometric design already well on its way to completion. *Kurt's started a project,* I thought. *All right!* But just as I unwound the paper in which the gift was packed, I saw the best part: peeking out at me were the words *I love you* woven into the warp in red letters.

What a darling idea. I cut that piece of fabric off the loom, glued it to a small bar of wood, and hung it in my studio. I look at it every day, and did so again not five minutes ago. For over thirty years that tiny wall hanging has silently called out Kurt's love over and over, across the decades and across the miles.

Every one of us has little opportunities each day to intentionally weave love into somebody else's life. Maybe it's through a note in a school lunch box for your son or daughter. Maybe it's a short message scribbled in the dust on top of the dresser before you leave for work. It might be a bouquet of flowers to thank someone for a kindness. What about a smile to your neighbor, a song over the phone, a prayer in someone's behalf? Once when Kurt visited me, he hid twenty little love notes all over the place where I found them for weeks after he left. All but the one he swears he put in the oven.

The point is, don't sit around waiting for the big knock-your-socks-off opportunity to say "I love you." It's the "little things" that really make a difference in the lives of those you love. Mother Teresa once said, "We ourselves feel that what we are doing is just a drop in the ocean. But if that drop was not in the ocean, I think the ocean would be less because of that missing drop. I do not agree with the big way of doing things."

I want to make that simple heart attitude and intentional giving of myself a part of the fabric of my daily living. How about you?

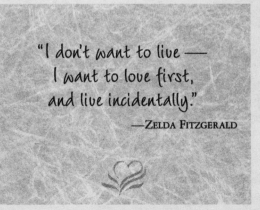

"I don't want to live —
I want to love first,
and live incidentally."

—Zelda Fitzgerald

Conclusion: You Are Loved!

~ Sheila Walsh

The six of us have the joy of meeting thousands of women every year as we speak at conferences across the country. Many stories and faces stay with us for a long time. We laugh and cry together as we marvel at the faithfulness of God in even the most heartbreaking of circumstances. We are all profoundly changed by the privilege God gives us to see his love at work in the lives of so many people who cross our path. Our prayer as we sat down to write this book to you was that you would know you are loved—boundlessly, fearlessly, stubbornly, lavishly, outlandishly, intentionally—by the God of the universe, the one who created you and calls you by name.

I will never forget a woman I met at the end of a Women of Faith conference in 1998. She looked to be about eighty years old. At first she couldn't talk to me; she simply held my hand and wept. She reminded me of my grandmother, and I took her in my arms and held her for a while. When she was able to speak, this is what she said:

"I've gone to church all my life. But this is the first time I really understood that God loves me. Not just everybody . . . but *me*. He really loves *me!*"

I thought about that woman a lot after that night. How would it have affected her life if she had understood as a child that she was profoundly loved by God? How would it affect all of our lives if we understood how passionately we are loved by God? I am convinced that we have captured only the smallest glimpse of who Christ really is. I am sure that when we are finally Home, we will be overwhelmed by how little we understood on earth.

Think of John, Christ's beloved disciple. He was perhaps the closest friend of Jesus on this earth. He was probably no more than eighteen years old when he became a disciple. He was the only one at the foot of the cross when Jesus was crucified. He was the second to arrive at the tomb after Christ had risen. He saw it all.

But as Scripture records the rest of John's journey through life, we find him many years later on the Isle of Patmos, a Roman penal colony, the Alcatraz of the Aegean Sea. He is seventy- five or eighty years old. He is near the end of his life, the end of his ministry, the end of the road. But God chose this man, at this moment in his life, to receive what we now know as "The Revelation"—the glorious picture of Christ's kingdom yet to come.

I used to think that if I had only been there with Christ, seen the dead raised with my own eyes, experienced the miracles, then my life would be different. Now I don't think so. John knew Christ as well as a human being could, but when he saw the vision of Christ fully revealed in all his risen glory John said, "When I saw him [Jesus], I fell at his feet as though dead. Then he placed his right hand on me and said: 'Do not be afraid. I am the First and the Last. I am the Living One; I was dead, and behold I am alive for ever and ever! And I hold the keys of death and Hades'" (Revelation 1:17–18).

My friends, we have not even begun to fathom the breadth and the length and the height and the depth of the love and majesty of God. He is the Alpha and Omega, the beginning and the end. Circumstances will not dictate the days of your life, God will. God, in his boundless love, will carry you safely Home into eternity in his glorious presence.

And so we wrap you up in a prayer of love and thanksgiving, and leave you with this immutable truth: You are loved. You are loved. You are loved!

Boundless Love

IS BASED ON THE POPULAR
WOMEN OF FAITH CONFERENCE.

WOMENᴏꜰFAITH™

Women of Faith partners with various
Christian organizations, including
Campus Crusade for Christ International,
Crossings Book Club,
Integrity Music, International Bible Society
Partnerships, Inc., and World Vision
to provide spiritual resources for women.

**For more information about Women of Faith
or to register for one of our nationwide
conferences, call 1-800-49-FAITH.**

www.womenoffaith.com

Women of Faith Devotionals

Joy Breaks
Hardcover 0-310-21345-2

We Brake for Joy!
Hardcover 0-310-22042-4
Audio Pages 0-310-22434-9

OverJoyed!
Hardcover 0-310-22653-8
Audio Pages 0-310-22760-7

Extravagant Grace
Hardcover 0-310-23125-6
Audio Pages 0-310-23126-4

Resources for Women of Faith℠

BOOKS/AUDIO

WOMEN OF FAITH BIBLE STUDY SERIES

WOMEN OF FAITH WOMEN OF THE BIBLE STUDY SERIES

WOMEN OF FAITH ZondervanGroupware™

*Inspirio's innovative and elegant gift books capture
the joy and encouragement that is an integral part of the
Women of Faith^{SM} movement.*

Joy for a Woman's Soul
Promises to Refresh Your Spirit
ISBN: 0-310-97717-7

Grace for a Woman's Soul
Reflections to Renew Your Spirit
ISBN: 0-310-97996-X

Simple Gifts
*Unwrapping the
Special Moments of
Everyday Life*
ISBN: 0-310-97811-4

Padded Hardcover
4 x 7
208 pages

*Verses from the New International Version of
the Bible have been collected into this volume
to inspire Women of Faith^{SM}
on their spiritual journey.*

Prayers for a Woman of Faith^{SM}
ISBN: 0-310-97336-8

Hardcover
5-1/4 x 5-1/4
128 pages

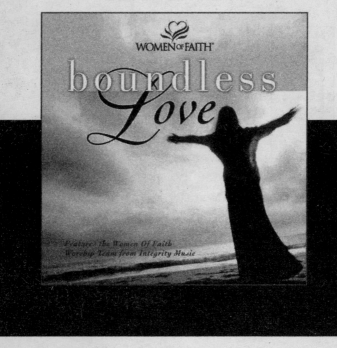